FOR MY GOOD

The story of the destiny chaser who, after controlling personal and structural confounders and conducting bias analyses, found significance in the relationship between relentless pursuits and the non-negotiable.

Karen Andrea Armstrong, PhD, MPH

Trilogy Christian Publishers

A Wholly Owned Subsidary of Trinity Broadcasting Network

2442 Michelle Drive

Tustin, CA 92780

For information, address Trilogy Christian Publishing

Rights Department, 2442 Michelle Drive, Tustin, Ca 92780.

For information about special discounts for bulk purchases, please contact Trilogy Christian Publishing.

Manufactured in the United States of America

10 9 8 7 6 5 4 3 2 1

Library of Congress Cataloging-in-Publication Data is available.

B-ISBN#: 978-1-64773-408-4

E-ISBN#: 978-1-64773-409-1

Dedication

To God be the glory, great things He has done! Thank you, God, that in the spiritual and temporal deserts—the times when I felt hidden, lost, and stagnant—you were pruning and growing me for the perfect time, the perfect destiny!

I dedicate this book to my amazing parents, Arthur and Mable Smith—you are gone, but always in my heart—and to my wonderful sisters and brothers. Thank you for your unconditional love and unparalleled support. I am forever grateful for the lessons of love and the rich milieu, the atmosphere of confidence and spiritual abundance which you provided for me and which continually buoys me up!

I dedicate this book to my beloved husband Winston; my phenomenal children, Shenelle, Shane, and stepdaughter, Danae; and to my vast extended family.

Thank you, family, for your unmatched support and unconditional love. I could not have written this book without you! You always believed in me and were willing to cheer me on, in and out of the spotlight! I love you and cherish you!

Foreword

As one of my family members recounted, I raced through life with inimitable charm, interspersed with nonnegotiable faith! I was unstoppable—I was indefatigable! She stated that when I spoke, you knew that there was something special about me. An older sister described it as "star quality." She describes me as the little girl with the extra digits who boldly confronted the odds! The unique packaging...

The surprising belly laugh, refusing to be contained, bursting from the diminutive body when you least expected it. I was never afraid to laugh at myself—I was often self-deprecating as I laughed along with my siblings at my *then* little body and big head.

My *big head* surprisingly maintained equilibrium as it balanced on my diminutive frame. For a long time, I did not appear to be my chronological age—my playmates and siblings often teased me. Not fazed, I always had a quick comeback! My favorite retort: "Yeah, big head, but full of brains!" I was not wrong, as people often praised me and spoke about how bright, smart, and sharp I was! Of course, I say this with modesty and humility. Despite the demure aura, the petite stature, and the small frame, I stood tall intellectually and academically. I also proved to be emotionally strong and immensely courageous.

I was told that I was a gifted child before I even knew what the term meant. In fact, from an early age, my family tells me that I disarmed everyone with my quiet confidence, my effervescent personality, my infectious laughter, and a captivating smile. Paradoxically, this demonstrable or professed introvert invariably shunned the limelight, but destiny thrust her center stage with her notable accomplishments. To God be all glory, honor, and praise!

Preface

Research Proposal

I am embarking on an ambitious undertaking by using research methodology as a metaphorical backdrop, applied to my life's journey. Over my life's course I have personally and professionally conducted more than 10,000 hours of scientific research, so indeed that makes me an expert researcher (Gladwell 2000). I have collaborated on multi-disciplinary research, and my findings have been presented at national and international conferences and published in peer-reviewed journals. I have served as research program director for a prestigious research university. Moreover, I have worked in research enterprises encompassing palliative care, brain health/neurology, medical-surgical, oncology, cardiology, gerontology, and epidemiology.

My instincts tell me that I should approach my life study using a qualitative research grounding, utilizing an inductive approach as best practice. I am biased as a quantitative researcher, so I will use an inferential approach, figuratively speaking, to explore my life's case study. Thus, as the primary researcher and my *only* study participant, I will use subjective and objective data to interpret study findings, of course using myself as the study instrument. I crave your indulgence as I attempt to describe the structures of my experiences as they elucidated my consciousness.

A renowned scientist once stated that "everything that can be counted does not necessarily count; everything that counts cannot necessarily be counted" (Einstein n.d.). Therefore, I will borrow ethnographic and phenomenological methodology and focus my life study on constructs derived from field observation of sociocultural phenomena. I plan to use a systematic collection and objective evaluation of data related to my past occurrences in order to test my hypotheses concerning the causes, effects, or trends of these events that may help to explain present events and anticipate future events (Creswell 2016) (Gay 1996).

My goal is to share my story in order to inspire others and to openly testify of God's goodness and unfailing mercy in my life. I am not worthy or deserving, but God chose to use me, a simple, ordinary woman, to do something extraordinary. Allow me to put on my epidemiologist hat as I hypothesize that there is a significant relationship between ordinary people who align themselves with God's power and the uncommon faith to accomplish extraordinary things.

I invite you to travel with me as I share my story of redemption and restoration—a path sprinkled with petals of paralyzing fear, blood-curdling heartbreak, numbing disappointment, delayed destiny, shocking perseverance, spontaneous bravery, and unwavering faith to reach my destination, dripping with succulent triumph! The bumps in the road were only commas, not periods! The detours only delayed my destiny; they did not deny it. Despite the fast and furious curveballs coming at me at over one hundred miles per hour, I managed to *fall* but not *yield*. My story is about reclaiming my destiny—moving from transition to transcendence, from recrimination to restoration and redemption.

As I attempt to encapsulate my inspirational, timely, relevant, and poignant life story into 160-plus pages, I can't help but be moved to tears as I reflect on the trajectory of my life—where God brought me from hurt, lack, brokenness, and interrupted destiny to where I am currently. The dark times, the hard times, the brokenness, the failures, the successes, and the triumphs were part of God's master plan. My story reverberates with courage and resilience and shows the power of non-negotiable faith in a God who orchestrated His plans for me in utero! Indeed, all things worked together *for my good!*

Acknowledgments

First, I thank God for His faithfulness and guidance as He helped me to complete this manuscript. I thank God for loving me regardless of my shortcomings. I give God thanks for His goodness, favor, and blessings. He propelled me past my fears and helped me challenge the assumptions. He sheltered and protected me from the storms of life. He has led me perfectly, ordered my steps, supplied every need, shepherded me, and covered me under His wings. He reminds me that He knows my name, He numbers the hairs on my head, and He sees me. I have kept God at my center. He is my Rock, Source, Healer, and Provider. My faith has been tested and tried in ways I cannot articulate. But, in all that I have been through, God has been my constant. Thus, the journey has been worth it! I can say, like the apostle Paul: "...*without faith it is impossible to please Him!*"[i]

I would like to acknowledge my wonderful God-fearing parents, siblings, and vast extended family. I would like to acknowledge my spiritual leaders who have guided and nurtured me through the years. I owe you a debt of gratitude. I appreciate your prayers, care, concern, mentorship, and support throughout this journey.

I would like to acknowledge my editor, publication team members, and the TBN family: you were there for me in the darkness and helped me to emerge with brilliance. In the dark times, your programs were a source of comfort and inspiration day and night. I recall watching one program, over thirty years ago, where a renowned speaker testified about her healing from cancer. Her testimony gave me the confidence and courage to discard my presumed *lifetime* prescription medications. I told myself that if God could heal cancer, He could take care of my heart problem. It is only fitting that almost thirty years later, TBN was instrumental in the publication of this work. Thank you, TBN!

I would like to express my sincere appreciation and heartfelt thanks to my mentors, past and present. You started me on my career trajectory—I will always be grateful for your guidance and mentorship. Thank you!

Thank you to my dear friends and colleagues: I owe you a debt of gratitude for your generosity and caring spirit. I am so glad that our paths crossed. You inspired me to relentlessly pursue excellence. I am grateful for the partnerships and collaborations. To my students and "mentees," your dedication is unmatched. You inspire me with your courage and perseverance. I am so proud of the next generation of nurse leaders. You will do great things!

Last, but certainly not least, I acknowledge my beloved husband and soulmate, Winston, without whose love, commitment, and devotion this book would not be possible. I acknowledge my phenomenal children, Shenelle and Shane, my cheerleaders and critics, who keep me humble and grounded. I acknowledge my wonderful stepdaughter, Danae, and my amazing nieces, nephews, cousins, in-laws, and other extended family. *Truly, all things work together for our good!* To God be the glory!

Introduction

Life Course Research Plan

Study Design

The researcher must use an adequate sample size for a study to demonstrate that differences or relationships exist. Determining sample size encompasses the use of calculations that include statistical power, alpha/significance level, and effect size (Grove et al., 2013). My study is ambitious—I am using a sample size of one: myself. I will attempt to prove that my life study is supernaturally overpowered by virtue of my alignment with God, undergirded by non-negotiable faith.

The Essence of Non-negotiable Faith

I walked away from the blackness, stepped out of the darkness, was unceremoniously lifted into the light. I acquiesced to the gentle promptings, propelled by a strength I did not recognize. I surrendered with outstretched arms opened wide, inspired by the newfound awareness that the struggles, stumbling blocks, pitfalls, and setbacks were all blessings in disguise. I humbly bowed in reverence to the omnipotent, omnipresent, omniscient God who teaches me that "...I can do all things through Christ who strengthens me!"[ii]

Moving in faith and trusting God, I made the tough decision to leave a lucrative job. I was experiencing cognitive dissonance—I refused to be part of the unethical behavior and unsound business practices. I walked away from the duplicity, the venom, the toxicity, the negativity. I bristled at the lack of support, the ingratitude, and the withheld validation. I made one move and provoked a tsunami of blessings and re-positioning beyond my wildest dreams. Little things do have the power to make a big difference (Gladwell 2000). I had reached my tipping point.

I was stifling yet again—when would the cycle end? Once again, I found myself in a desperate place—I knew that I must distance myself from the saboteurs, the demons, the manipulation. I recoiled from the subterfuge, the missing ethos, the phoniness. The disingenuous platitudes were empty-sounding brass and tinkling cymbals. Non-negotiable! I refused to be bullied, I refused to let my spirit drown, and I refused to let my psyche be crushed. I wanted my peace back!

Despite the well-meaning "It's not the right time! Your job here is not finished..." No. My season was over! I would not overstay the welcome. My purpose in that relationship was fulfilled. My heart responded in perfect cadence. It was time. I did not see it at the time, but this move proved to be providential. I refused to be complicit with the dishonesty and unethical practices—that was my non-negotiable!

Ethnographical Data

The Master Designer, Architect of My Faith

From almost severing my tongue at six years old to being valedictorian twice; from a college dropout to becoming a perpetual student earning two bachelor's degrees, two master's degrees, and a PhD; from college professor to dean of academic programs; from nursing assistant to Chief Nursing Administrator; from almost barren to mother of two; from abusive relationships to a fulfilled marriage of over twenty-seven years; from violation to restoration! I stand in awe of God's love, faithfulness, and mercy toward me. I persevered and emerged victorious. I know that God has a master plan for my life, and that He came to give me hope and a future.[iii] Moreover, the Bible states that I am more than conqueror through Christ.[iv]

I now realize that all things work together *for my good!*[v] The giants came and fell... they revealed my strong character; they did not defeat me. The mountains did not stop me—they revealed God's influence, power, platform, and my drive, discipline, strength, and ultimate purpose, which is to reveal and reflect the goodness and faithfulness of God.

Giants come for us to be anointed and appointed, and to bring us to places of influence and power, as we take our rightful place in our spheres of influence (Jakes n.d.). I am the *destiny chaser* who got my one moment in time to be all that I could be when I faced and slayed my Goliaths and waltzed into my destiny, singing redemption songs—songs of freedom—and resonating with restoration as I reflect on my journey of faith and redemption, knowing that all things worked together *for my good!*

I move into my new chapter, albeit with the fortuitous undergirded by the providential. I am realigning my priorities, refusing to be tolerated, confidently demanding celebration, seeking the sunshine, the light, the beauty in miracles, the deliverance, the redemption, the second chance—I found the road less traveled. I am coming up for air, filling my lungs with renewed faith and purpose. Optimistic for my future. I emerge energized, refreshed, and poised for flight.

Taking a deep breath, emerging from the abyss—excitement threatening to lift me off the ground. Buoyed up by supernatural wings and surrounded by indescribable peace. Held up by invisible, strong hands of mercy and grace. Defying gravity with a pull so great! Finding the beauty in the ashes, rising like the phoenix, embracing renewed purpose—filling my lungs with joy, rebirth, renaissance, a shift in thinking, alignment with the stars, and reverberating, unwavering faith. I walk into my fresh start, my "millionth second chance," my new beginning, my new chapter. No, not fortuitous—providential!

God, thank You for the rough spots. Thank You for allowing me to confront the non-negotiable and to overcome the tears, pain, abuse, and betrayal. The weapons were formed, but did not prosper; they could not contain this fighting spirit—the resilience. I could not have imagined how God would bless me exceedingly abundantly above all I could ever ask or think. The finishing of what God started decades ago... providential! I have learned that *with God, all things are possible!*[vi]

I am rejecting the null! The null hypothesis is undertheorized—I aim to explain it in a spiritual context. I am spurning the bad, the ugly, the uncomfortable, the negative, the limiting, the lousy!

Null: Negative, Uncomfortable, Limiting, Lousy.

I am accepting the *Alternative: the Audacious, Limitless, Triumphant, Enduring, Relentless, Non-negotiable, Astronomical, Transformational, Indestructible, Victorious, and Excellent!*

I am claiming God's fierce, supernatural, unfathomable, unmeritable favor! I find a new purpose undergirded by faith that defies logic. Inexplicable, unreasonable, latent faith. The panacea, the prescription for fulfilling my purpose with relentless favor. Unwavering faith that defies logic! In my journey of faith and fulfillment, finding that hidden purpose and fulfilling my ultimate dream, purpose, and passion. I believe that whatever my mind conceives, it will achieve. I believe that God's will supersedes everything in my life![vii]

Further, I know that God is in control of all my affairs, that He is the arbiter of my faith, and that He determines my destiny.[viii] Moreover, as I find God's purpose for my life, I am reminded that God has the final say. I found confirmation in overcoming obstacles, refusing to settle, refusing to buy into the naysayers and haters. I refused to accept when the teacher said no, the professor said no, leadership said no, the numbers said no, the doctor said lifelong medication. Now, finding inner peace, believing in the impossible, refusing to settle, refusing to quit, surmounting the obstacles to get to the path of resilience, restoration, and redemption.

Trusting the still, small voice, destined to find faith, favor, and determination in the journey of transition and transcendence. Knowing that God cares for us no matter how imperfect or unloving we may be.[ix] The One who threw the stars in space and holds the world in the palm of His hands—the One who allows me to defy the odds, navigate the ivory towers of academia, break through the glass ceiling, confront corporate greed, and address unethical behaviors. Finding a new passion and the anointed and appointed purpose, fulfilling the dream by taking the road less traveled, trusting in the higher power, believing in something bigger than me... knowing that God has equipped me for something bigger.

According to (White n.d.) "When every other voice is hushed, and in quietness we wait before Him, the silence of the soul makes more distinct the voice of God." I discovered that by listening to the still, small voice of God, I have successfully chased my destiny and emerged triumphant. I have refused to be defined by the hidden, dark places. I am constantly overcoming the relentless pull on my psyche; foraging through and overcoming obstacles; seeing the invisible; tasting the success; trusting myself; and most importantly, trusting the One who knows the end from the beginning! Inspiring positive change, making my mark in the world, serving others with unquenchable faith, and capitalizing on the determination to fulfill my destiny and purpose, one dream at a time, one person at a time!

Contents

Prologue

Rejecting the Null

It is well established that researchers often study the dynamic interplay of social determinants of health to create interventions and promote positive health outcomes (Northridge 2004) and (Earp 2012). Moreover, researchers often test for significant relationships among certain variables, create awareness, and stir consciousness in their attempts to answer troubling questions. Researchers explore mechanisms of behaviors, and illuminate and explain elusive and spurious relationships among diseases and conditions that affect us globally (Earp 2012).

Similarly, quantitative researchers aim to accurately *reject the null hypothesis* in their conclusions about significant relationships. To avoid certain types of errors, researchers must be careful *not to reject a null hypothesis that is true* (Frankfort 2008). Thus, they may conduct bias analyses, to control for confounders or extraneous variables, and report scientific findings with more certainty.

After conducting a *bias analysis* to address potential threats to the validity of my life study, I am proud to report that, conditional on the accuracy of my *bias-adjusted model,* as a destiny chaser with God's authority, I found a significant relationship among my life variables, God's influence, favor, and supernatural anointing and appointing. Using non-negotiable faith, I arrived at a place of victory and indescribable peace.

Gerontological Approaches

Over the trajectory of my career and lived experiences, I have come to the unequivocal conclusion that God uses ordinary people to do extraordinary things. In fact, I am convinced that God often uses people who are imperfect and undeserving but willing and available to be used by Him. Moreover, when we remain willing and open, obstacles often arise to try to hinder our progress and thwart God's plans for our lives. Hence, the weapons of spiritual warfare may be deployed against me, but they will not prosper.[x] Thus, we must be willing to be humble, strong, vulnerable, patient, and transparent in order for God to fulfill His purpose in our lives.

Study Objective

The Master Designer, Architect of My Faith

The study objective is to identify and understand the personal and structural factors that led me to submission to God's will and purpose for my life. My goal is to share my life story in order to inspire others and to openly testify of God's goodness and unfailing mercy in my life. I am not worthy or deserving, but God chose to use me, a simple woman, to show that nothing is impossible when we trust God. My story reverberates with resilience—the power of non-negotiable faith in a God who orchestrated plans for me in utero!

Research Question/Hypothesis

My research question is: Do all things work together *for my good?* My hypothesis is that there is a significant relationship between ordinary people who align themselves with God's power and the ability to accomplish extraordinary things.

Variables of Interest

My life study variables are biological, sociological, structural, and behavioral factors, and levels of spirituality. The important mediating, moderating, and/or confounding variables are fruits of the Spirit, non-negotiable faith, and trust in God. Moderators include age group, ethnicity, multiple exposures, and individual risk factors.

Independent variables: the independent variables, or variables that are manipulated, include but are not limited to: i) faith, ii) patience, iii) obedience, and iv) trust. *Dependent variables:* the dependent variables or outcome variables are faith, victory, and ultimate disposition of God's master plan for my life.

I aim to find the relationship between faith and victory, embracing the inconceivable and accepting God's challenge to trust the plan of the master Teacher. The ultimate victory is mine! I am cognizant of the fact that opposition is my opportunity. I know that God will do something bigger than me—and most importantly, I know that when God is doing something for me, spiritual weapons of warfare may be deployed, but they will not prosper![xi] What God has for me—it is for *me*! I may not have always come up through the ranks, but God has placed me strategically and providentially where He wants me, when He wants!

Observations

Ethical Considerations

We face ethical dilemmas every day, and what do we do when we face ethical dilemmas? We take mental shortcuts or heuristics. We take the easy way out. We all know that we should not make *the perfect the enemy of the good,* but we run blindly into cognitive dissonance. Oh, yes! We're all guilty of the *fundamental attribution error* (Ross 1991)—when somebody does something socially undesirable, we judge them, but when we are faced with the same ethical dilemma, we justify our behaviors; we find reasons to rationalize why we react, why we do certain things. The fact of the matter is, what you think of me is none of my business, and what I think of you is none of your business, because people often operate with limited information. So, we should not judge others or make spurious conclusions.

Assumptions

We often make flawed assumptions, because at any given moment, we do not have all the facts—it is like the well-documented optical illusion of the ugly old lady and the beautiful young woman juxtaposed on each other. In one instant, while you see an old, withered, ugly lady, someone else is looking at the same picture and sees a young, beautiful woman. So, you are both right; it all depends on the point of view or perspective. Both frames of reference are equally valuable and deserving of respect.

I want to say thank you for your dedication, for your commitment, for not judging me when I did not always get it right—but when we know better, we do better! (Angelou n.d.). Let us respect each other and continue to practice the golden rule of doing to others what we want done to us! When we gossip, when we pick away or malign people's characters, it doesn't make us better by making someone else look small!

When I look back and connect the dots as to what has been most fulfilling, most purposeful in my life, only then will I be able to understand the detours and ultimately find my true purpose in life. It is well-documented that we must be intentional about finding our life's purpose. For example, when we are creative, kind, receptive, abundant, and beautiful, that is when we find the best desires (Dyer n.d.). With God at the center, when we are living for others and being more community-oriented and altruistic, we find equanimity and balance in our lives—and true happiness and joy!

Part 1

Historical, Phenomenological, and Sociological Data

Chapter 1

In the Beginning

Jamaica: the island in the sun, 1,721 miles from the United States with 1,411 square miles of white, sandy beaches and a kaleidoscope of variegated plumes, exotic fruits, happy smiles, and bright sunshine. Home of reggae great Bob Marley; long distance runners like Merlene Ottey; the notorious bobsled team; national hero Marcus Garvey; nurse Mary Seacole; and the fastest man alive, Usain Bolt. The list goes on...

The lyrics of a popular reggae classic by the prolific songwriter (Marley n.d.) reverberate in my head: "Emancipate yourself from mental slavery/None but ourselves can free our minds!"

Sampling Strategy

The Early Life-course

My family tells me: "On a warm January morning, a beautiful baby girl was born to joyful parents on the island paradise of Jamaica." The ninth of thirteen children, I am told that I was the apple of my parents' eyes. This dubious honor is often challenged by a certain sibling. I was perfect in every way, except I had twelve fingers and ten toes. Maybe there was something special about the exotic creature with large, brown, almond-shaped eyes. My features have certainly changed over the years!

Siblings later regaled family with stories about how spoilt I was and how our parents failed to discipline me—they claim I got away with everything, disarmed everyone with my cuteness, was mischievous, petite, and smart. I was undoubtedly unique—from an early age I was a standout, and clearly destined for greatness! In fact, in high school I was voted "most likely to succeed" by peers and faculty.

According to *The Power of Intention*, anything we can conceive and believe, while staying in harmony with the universal, all-creating source, can and must come to pass (Dyer n.d.)! So, I invite you to boldly step forward and claim all that God has in store for you. Identify the non-negotiable! Confidently embark on the faith-filled journey by aligning yourself with the omnipotent, omniscient source of all good things, the Almighty God!

Meta Data

We should not put our confidence in our talents, mental or physical prowess, spiritual or educational training—we can only place our confidence in God, the source of all gifts and blessings. The apostle Paul tells us that he counts all things as loss except for the excellence of the knowledge of Jesus Christ, and that we should forget the things that are behind us and press toward the mark of the high calling of God in Christ![xii] Further, we lose the anointing whenever we put our confidence in our talents, training, accomplishments, or gifts. Instead, we must depend on God, and by so doing, we receive His grace and allow His light to shine through us. God wants us to be completely dependent upon Him. All that we are, and everything that we have accomplished, we could only have done through Christ. Thus, we should only be confident in God's blessings and the abilities that He has bestowed on us. Most of all, we must always rejoice, pray unceasingly, and give thanks in all circumstances![xiii]

Dancing with My Mother

I loved to dance! In primary school I participated in competitions. My mother loved to worship, sing, and dance. She danced along with all of her spiritual gospel music, and she did not hesitate to grab any unwilling partner who happened to be nearby. She did not like it when we listened to or sang "secular" or popular music. I fell in love with dancing from seeing my mother dance. To this day, I crack my family up with my moves—my children have threatened to release unauthorized video recordings of me dancing on social media if they do not get their way. Ouch!

Information Gathering

I am told that from an early age, I was intellectually curious. My two older sisters attended elementary school less than a quarter mile from home. Being the younger sibling, I had not reached school age. My sisters came home for lunch every day and walked the short distance back to school. I remember one day, I wanted to accompany my older siblings to school after they came home for lunch. Despite my mom's vocal disapproval, I followed my siblings back to school. When my mom discovered that I was missing, she came to the school and took me back home. I resisted and protested, to no avail. She spanked my little legs with a little switch all the way home as a reminder not to disobey her. So much for wanting to go to school prematurely!

Intervening Variable

Initiatives

I never went to pre-school—no, I went straight to second grade! I skipped pre-k, kindergarten, and first grade and went straight to the second grade. As I grew older, I also took the liberty of self-enrolling in a high school preparatory class. My older sister was legitimately enrolled in the course. I remember presumptuously sitting in on her high school preparatory classes. I was somewhat taken aback when the teacher asked me to leave. She stated that I was too young to take the common entrance exams which launched primary school students into high school. I had to wait another year to be eligible to sit the common entrance exams. Destiny delayed, not denied!

Subjective and Objective Data

All-Island Essay Competition Winner

My sixth-grade primary school teacher approached me one day. This was the year before I was supposed to go to high school. She remarked, "You're such a good writer, I think you should enter the all-island essay competition!" She mentioned that the national essay competition "Project Pull Together" related to citizens' proposals for improving outcomes for the disparate in the community—a harbinger of my dissertation topic many decades later.

A few months later, my teacher informed me that I was chosen to be the island winner of the essay competition. I appeared in the national newspaper and was invited to meet with the Member of Parliament at a luncheon in the Pegasus Hotel. My success was met with skepticism—my peers knew that I had several older siblings. My classmate scoffed, "Oh, your sister must've written the essay for you." The assertion was ridiculous, since my siblings had no idea that I had even entered this competition. My prize money was $300—a lot of money in those days. My father took it and invested it for me.

Over-achiever and Path to Excellence

The high school years were a chance for me to shine! Not only was I an "A" student, but my leadership skills were honed from an early age. I became the student council president, the Head Girl, and the only female on the school's challenge competition team, for which I represented our school on the national stage. I was also the only female in my advanced level science/junior college science classes, which were male dominated. As a result of being part of the scholastic team, I was on television, and my father was so proud of me. I remember him coming to get me from the bus stop when the school's challenge competition ended. I felt like a little celebrity in my neighborhood.

I graduated at the top of my class in high school and was selected to be class valedictorian. Similarly, when I graduated from advanced or "A" levels, similar to junior college, I was also valedictorian. I was awarded the principal's trophy for outstanding academic and leadership performance. I was voted by my peers as "most likely to succeed."

Correlations and Outliers

Talented and Gifted

My intellectual prowess appeared to dominate my peers. I was unstoppable! As a child, I studied the dictionary while my peers read novels and comic books. My vocabulary was always superior as compared to my counterparts. In high school, my English teacher told me that I had mastered the English language! I recall how she reprimanded me when she saw me reading a romance novel, literature she clearly considered *infra dig* for me. Further, I am proud to say, and no disrespect to my gender, but I was the *only* female in my junior college cohort enrolled in the advanced level science classes in biology, physics, chemistry, and mathematics. These college-level courses, formally known as the University of Cambridge International General Certificate of Education: Advanced Level, or Cambridge (GCE) A-Level(s), were graded by the University of Cambridge.

Chapter 2

Longitudinal Data

Winter

At times it seemed we had two generations living together in my childhood home, because my oldest sibling was fifteen years older than me. In a culture where colorism thrived, lighter-complexioned children were complimented in a back-handed fashion with terms like "red gal" and "pretty," while dark-skinned children were called "black boy" or the "black one." I am told that I was one of my parents' favorite, sometimes to my peril, by older, jealous siblings who playfully gave me a hard time! I say this facetiously!

My childhood revolved around the overarching theme of Christianity and faith. The way we comported ourselves, the way we dressed, and the food we ate all reverberated Seventh-day Adventism—we observed a weekly Sabbath. Every aspect, every conduit, every experience, no matter how mundane, was punctuated by faith. From an early age, my Christian values and beliefs dictated every move and decision.

Predictable Behaviors

We observed a Christian Sabbath, which means we paused and ignored anything secular from Friday sunset to Saturday sunset. On Wednesday nights, my parents designated it as prayer meeting night, so we could not watch television. Worship was pervasive in our home, almost *ad nauseam*—we had to get up at sunrise, and before we retired to bed each night, we were expected to participate in family worship—we yawned and slept through most of it.

My siblings and I always knew that were held to a higher standard, and we were governed by values and beliefs which were often incongruent with those of several school friends and neighbors.

Despite these idiosyncrasies, we were very popular in school.

From an early age, my parents instilled in me a sense of responsibility and community service—where every Monday morning on my way to primary school, my job was to deliver a gallon of milk to one of my mother's paying customers or as a gift to an indigent family. I was not a happy camper—I murmured and complained, but it later made me appreciate the simple things in life and value random acts of kindness. This weekly task made me responsible and mature. My work ethic was sculpted from an early age.

I also enjoyed a childhood full of laughter and fun. I was a very mischievous child. I played pranks on everyone, including my parents. My whole family knew that if they were walking into a room, they needed to be on their guard, because I could pop out of any corner and startle them! Moreover, if I felt the house was too quiet for my liking, I would retrieve the lid of my mom's largest and heaviest ironware pot, and I would just drop the heavy lid in the middle of a tile floor! The reverberation first startled, then annoyed, and then tickled everyone... and they knew it was me.

Chapter 3
Confidence Intervals

The Trifecta

From an early age, *my trifecta* was praise, prayer, and psalms-- the three Ps! Growing up in Jamaica we took so much for granted: the little courtesies, the kindness of strangers, the extended family—bloodline or not, the assumption that we are all equal. Not being afraid to say good morning or to pick up someone who was walking and needed a ride. It did take a village—a close-knit community where you took care of the less-fortunate, you felt free to talk to strangers, or children could safely play until sunset. The carefree exuberance, basking in the sunshine, walking on the beach. Like the saying goes, "No problem, mon!" Just an indescribable feeling of freedom, peace, and one love, as Bob Marley says: "One love, one heart/Let's get together and feel alright." I didn't fear the dark, or strangers, or walking alone. I felt nurtured, supported, and cared for. We celebrated our culture. We celebrated the relentless pursuit of excellence.

Imitation—the Best Form of Flattery

Despite the hand-me-downs and dresses which my mother masterfully crafted from drapery fabric, I wanted to be like my five older sisters. The sixth of seven girls in a tribe seasoned with six boys, I copied my older sisters in every way imaginable. It's ironic that now I want to be like my *little* sister, "when I grow up." I walked like my big sisters, spoke like them, dressed like them, read like them, danced, and sang songs as they often did. We loved watching TV, especially 20th Century Fox movies—I was overflowing with anticipation for Saturday night at the movies. When it was past our bedtime, we would lower the volume or darken the TV screen when our parents did their rounds after midnight. So, not surprisingly, when I was

29

about six years old, I had an accident while imitating my older sister, who jumped off the ledge effortlessly and landed on the driveway. I awkwardly tried to jump from the veranda ledge to the driveway. "Epic fail," as my children would say!

Interim Analyses:
Destiny Interrupted, but Not Denied

Severe and Adverse Event

After a couple of futile attempts, I missed the ledge and ignominiously landed on the driveway. To add insult to injury, midfall I must have clenched my teeth, because I somehow bit my tongue, and bit it hard! I started bleeding profusely from my mouth. Instantaneously, I felt a bolt of excruciating pain jolt through my body. When my sister investigated, she discovered that I had nearly severed my tongue. She screamed in horror.

My teeth had apparently cut my tongue to the point where I could not even speak. My father rushed me to the hospital, where I had to be given multiple stitches. The nurses and doctors somehow did not give me any anesthetic relief, and my father yelled at them for what he perceived to be inhumane treatment. However, my health care training now tells me that they wanted me to be conscious and alert while they stitched my tongue. I had to drink from a straw for many weeks because I could not eat while my tongue healed. This was an experience I will always remember.

Regressions to the Mean

I shudder to think how my life would have been different had I severed my tongue as a little girl, all those years ago! No feisty adolescent, no quick retort, no back-talk to my sisters who thought they were the boss of me as I navigated the teenage years, no Sabbath school secretary, no chorister, no youth leader, no debater, no school's challenge teammate, no Bible Bowler, no valedictorian, no student council president, no lecturer, no professor, no Chief Nurse Administrator, no friend or soulmate. The list goes on and on...Wow!

Oh, for a faith that would not shrink! Thank you, God, for the journey, for the path to this joy-centered life, and for this incredible career trajectory bounded by non-negotiable faith. A faith that has helped me to chase my destiny and to arrive victorious.

Chapter 4
Baseline Data

Humble Beginnings

Despite the humble beginnings, my siblings and I were well-liked and respected by our peers and colleagues. We were well-adjusted and confident young adults—we were well-respected, loved, and admired by everyone in the community. People frequently commented on how we all looked alike; you could tell we were all related. We were the first ones in our neighborhood with TVs and a telephone. In fact, I remember that when my older sister was a competitor in the Miss Jamaica beauty contest, our neighbors flocked to our home to watch the pageant.

Growing up, my father had trucks for his commercial business. He also owned a "clunker," which he loved—it was a loud, big, ugly sedan with fishtail bumpers. How we detested it! Since the older children only hung out with cool kids, we were embarrassed to be seen in the "dinosaur car."

Pretty soon, my sisters and I realized that it was more socially desirable to arrive by taxi or even to walk versus arriving in my dad's clunker, which you could hear approaching from a mile away. As a result, we decided to transfer our membership to the humble satellite church instead of maintaining our membership at the beautiful mother church, because the satellite church was within walking distance of our home. Thus, we avoided the stress of rushing to get ready in time to travel with my dad, who detested tardiness. In fact, it was commonplace for our dad to drive away without us if we failed to make his designated departure time. He would often leave us at home if we were late and not dressed by the appointed time.

Generational Influences

Family Ties

My family is always at the center of my joy. My siblings and I knew that we had a safe place; we knew that we were loved and cared for, no matter how humble the beginnings. One of my quirks as a little child was that I loved anything with sugar, and I was a picky eater—I only ate the protein in my meals. My brothers would wait for me to start my meal, and then they would grab my plate which, invariably, was barely touched. I only liked one form of carbohydrate—dumplings, in any form.

Being very petite and one of the younger girls, my dresses were invariably the product of leftover fabric from curtains and drapery. Moreover, it was not unusual for my sisters and I to have the same exact dresses. My older siblings knew that this was not "cool." My older sisters would coordinate amongst themselves to ensure that they would not be wearing the same dresses for the same occasion. They failed to include me in the "meetings" about what dress to wear and when. However, being the youngest girl then, I would welcome the opportunity to be in matching outfits with my sisters—being a mischievous imp and maybe lacking self-awareness, I would just wait until the last minute to see what my older sisters were wearing and then I would put my matching dress on, to their chagrin.

I was insecure about my physique from an early age. I was very petite, with very muscular arms and angular lines. I overheard some students calling me "underdeveloped" because I must have been the last girl to develop breasts in high school. Hence, some of my classmates were unforgiving and teased me mercilessly; I later received the name "FBI" or "flat-breasted individual."

Fast-forward to thirty-five years later—I am very proud of my voluptuous curves, which surfaced mysteriously over the years. God truly has a sense of humor, and I eventually got my share of curves in middle age. Notwithstanding, I have days where I wish I could eat anything and not worry about gaining weight—I sometimes reminisce about my lithe frame with the awesome muscle tone that I inherited from my dad. He always bragged about his beautiful legs, up unto his death at ninety-two years old!

Secondary Analysis

During the teenage years, I found myself moving up into the upper echelon of society. I would often associate with persons who were economically more well-situated, by virtue of my older sister's social connections. After graduating from sixth form /junior college, I took some time off to live with one of my older sisters and her family. I moved to a more affluent neighborhood within walking distance of the beach. I felt like the "Fresh Prince(ss) of Bel-Air." This older sister has exceptional business acumen. She has done well for herself. When I lived with her, I had a *nice* life. I recall the times when my cotton nightgowns were ironed, and my bed linens meticulously laundered and ironed; when breakfast was always waiting downstairs—not finger foods or sandwiches, but exquisite meals consumed with fine cutlery on mahogany tables covered with crisp linen tablecloths. As a result of the social circles I moved in, I always had a car waiting to take me wherever I needed to go. Before immigrating to the Unites States, I enjoyed an upper-middle class social economic status.

Cross-sectional Data

Formative Years

Paradoxically, as a young girl, it was incredible that I grew up not being aware that I was *poor* by earthly standards. Notwithstanding, I was blessed with rich inner experiences that molded and shaped my childhood. I always felt confident and empowered in the formative years. In my naivete, I felt free to be whomever I chose to be. The sky was the limit. I dared to dream and to think big. I have now come to the realization that I am not unique in my family psychology. My close friends and counterparts often experienced similar idiosyncrasies as my family. Albeit, I felt like my family consisted of two generations of siblings, and I was precariously wedged between both. I had siblings who were sixteen years older than me and seemed lightyears away in maturity and swag; meanwhile, my youngest sibling was eight years younger than me.

I just remember being in a very happy home filled with joy, laughter, and mischief. I am sure my older siblings' perception did not align with mine as they later shared that, growing up, they often wished my parents had used more aggressive contraceptive protocols. My older siblings confessed that they were embarrassed with each new mouth to feed and care for, no matter how beautiful we were. They sheepishly shared that the little ones were such "beautiful babies." My mother later confided that she had tried various contraceptive methods but experienced challenges with the devices that were available to her back then. I have grown to love and appreciate my enormous family. I would not trade my humongous family for the world!

Because my father reared cows, goats, and chickens, plus cultivated a multitude of ground provisions, the staples in our diet were cows' milk, a plethora of vegetables, and assorted meats, excluding pork and crustaceans (consistent with our religious persuasions). My father had many acres of verdant soil in his family estate. My father also successfully acquired various government contracts and business agreements for which he hauled construction materials; unbeknownst to me, at the time, my father was an entrepreneur. My mom was quite the homemaker, dressmaker, financial manager, interior designer, counselor, and midwife to many neighbors. She was an informal gerontologist, taking care of the older people in the neighborhood. She was an informal epidemiologist, practicing complementary and alternative medicine—she was skilled in herbal remedies and immersed in meditation and the non-negotiable prayer of faith. She embodied the spirit of volunteerism and left our family a rich legacy of selfless service.

My mom took care of the alcoholic, the abused, the downtrodden, the man with Parkinson's disease, those suffering from dementia, abandoned babies, the homeless, and the orphans. My mom was the community health worker; she strategized, organizing her version of "Habitat for Humanity," building a home for an indigent old woman.

She was quite the businesswoman, marketing cows' milk, chickens, and vegetables from the back of the hilltop. She was quite the investor and taught me from an early age the power of multiple streams of income and increasing returns on investment. Mom would make the most beautiful and intricate curtains and drapes and, invariably, the remainder of fabric would be magically transformed into dresses for my older sisters and me. She even made the uniforms we wore to school.

Interactions

The Prankster

As my family recounts, I pranked everyone, so much so that growing up in the same household, my siblings had their antennas up when they knew I was at home. They never knew from which direction the prank would come. No telling whose juicy novel would disappear when they were in the middle of a delicious chapter; whose belongings would mysteriously disappear or be curiously misplaced at the most inopportune time; which siblings' lunch money would be diverted; whose chores sabotaged in cruel jest. In fact, my favorite prank was to hide behind doors, then jump out and startle any and everyone.

Part 2

Frames of Reference

Chapter 5
Concept Mapping

Coming to America

Juxtapose that past life with coming to America—riding in dirty subways, rubbing shoulders with everyone from the homeless person soaking in their own bodily fluids to the Wall Street executive—this really was culture shock, indeed. In later years, when my children would visit Jamaica, they were amazed at the abundant life I had traded for my newfound home. Not the shanty towns and depravity that our senses are assaulted with from news channels, documentaries, and social media. Sure, Jamaica is a developing country, economically stratified with distinguishable social classes, but not every immigrant is running from poverty and lack when immigrating to the United States.

Change Theory

I immigrated to New York and matriculated to Hunter College in Manhattan. After a horrendous commute, I took a break from school and ended up working as a bookkeeper at an upscale furrier, travelling back and forth to New York City. The animal activists eviscerated the company. However, by that time I had already acquired a beautiful fur coat at cost!

After some unfortunate circumstances I relocated to another state, where I embarked on a career of finance and credit management, at which I was successful. I refused to take residence or stay in careers where my talents were tolerated, *not* celebrated! In later years, when confronted by incivility and intolerance among peers and colleagues, I confidently subscribed to the words so exquisitely penned by Marianne Williamson: "Our greatest fear is not that we are inadequate, but that we are powerful beyond measure."

Sociological Perspective

Consciousness Raising

Arriving at JFK airport on a brutally cold, rainy Halloween night, my island blood was no match for the unrelenting, frigid temperatures. I disembarked with trepidation, unsure of my future. I was overwhelmed with mixed emotions and thoughts of what I had gotten myself into. The harsh winds hit my face. The blaring horns and loud pedestrians jaywalking jarred me back from my reverie. What *had* I gotten myself into? I walked into danger with my eyes wide open.

I trembled with uncertainty, greeted by rude trick-or-treaters throwing eggs at unassuming New York passersby. This was not how I imagined my arrival in the "city that never sleeps"—I came to fulfill my American dream, to get my pie in the sky. As my naïve twenty-three-year-old mind absorbed the culture shock of leaving my island paradise to acclimate to the notoriously rough New York City, my security blanket unceremoniously evaporated as I was thrust into the brutal reality of the city.

Social Constructs

I had immigrated to New York with the ultimate dream of pursuing medical school. I was excited about my new marriage and the promise of a great future. However, my excitement was short-lived. My joy was eclipsed by momentary glimpses of infidelity and duplicity. Something was terribly wrong, and I was afraid to share my misgivings. When family and friends inquired about my well-being, I pretended everything was fine. However, I could not shake the nagging feeling that my "house of cards" was about to about to crumble. My gut instincts were spot on.

My world was about to come crashing down on me. I felt lost and uncertain about my future. I felt trapped in the big city where everything was new and strange. I was nostalgic. I grieved the broken cultures, the pathology palpable in the broken psyches, the broken souls, the pervasive disparities. I felt the tensions, the subtle and covert racism—I was in culture shock.

In Jamaica we were insulated from prejudice despite the many ethnicities and our share of races. Like the United States, our national motto was *"E Pluribus Unum,"* meaning "Out of Many, One People"! However, in Jamaica, I never felt like a second-class citizen.

Chapter 6

Determinants of Health

Upstream Effects

People would sometimes remark, "What a beautiful accent!" or ask, "Where are you from?" I have come to realize that these phrases are intended to draw attention to racial differences in the form of *emic vs etic*, insider versus outsider. The converse may also be true, based on the proliferation of *implicit bias* studies (Blanton and Ikizer 2019). I have grown accustomed to this kind of interaction. I recall going on interviews, and when the human resources (HR) person came to greet me in the lobby, they avoided eye contact and seemed off-put when they realized I was black. Some people even remarked that I sounded white on the phone, plus my last name added to the confusion and highlighted the fact that I was an immigrant—albeit a proud and confident one!

Through a series of unfortunate circumstances, my dreams were thwarted. My destiny was delayed, but ultimately not denied. I believe that my story will inspire others to persevere despite adversity, to defy the odds, to rise from obscurity, discrimination, and brokenness, and to triumph as an overcomer. I hope that my story inspires others to never give up, to never settle, and to persist against all odds.

Transitions

Behavior Modifications

I have braved and overcome insurmountable odds to capture elusive success. I am a survivor! I have survived broken dreams, a bad marriage, a spontaneous miscarriage, and abusive relationships. I have finally found peace and triumph through divine intervention and providence.

How the script has changed—the story has been rewritten many times. Over thirty years ago—back then, in my finite mind—I could not envision a happy ending to a marriage which should never have taken place. So much had happened in a short space of time—a spontaneous miscarriage, dreams deferred, and thwarted plans of going to medical school; moving from privileged status to anonymity, from beloved to reproached, from faithful to doubtful, from bountiful to barren, from full of potential to bankrupt and broken. The nightmare had just begun.

Journey of Faith

Despite my difficult journey and transition to transcendence, I was able to accomplish much personally and professionally against the backdrop of a woman who had survived incredible odds—from almost having my tongue severed at six years old to being valedictorian twice; from nursing assistant to Chief Nursing Administrator; from patient care technician (PCT) to PhD (Doctor of Philosophy); from abusive relationships and spontaneous miscarriage to accomplished wife and mother; from having a cardiovascular anomaly which should have left me on lifetime medications—but by prayer and faith I was able to discard the medications, and I have been restored to normal cardiovascular health!

Cognitive Dissonance

I confronted the demons. I faced each grueling challenge with optimism, fortitude, and characteristic faith. I am buoyed by faith in the One who holds the future—the One who holds the world in place, hung the stars in space, counts all my teardrops, and puts them in a bottle.

I reached deep down inside my invisible bag of tools and immersed myself in my panacea—my trifecta—praise, prayer, and psalms! I have overcome insurmountable obstacles by divine providence. I say this with humility, for emphasis, and not to boast: With aggressive foresight and forward thinking, I earned my first bachelor's degree in three years, my second bachelor's degree in eighteen months concurrently with my first master's degree, then successfully completed a second master's degree at a top-rate research university. I completed my PhD in two and a half years (something of a feat!) and was offered a postdoctoral fellowship from a prestigious university. I accomplished all of this while working full time and raising a family.

After several lucrative jobs, I took the risk of walking away from a position that stifled me and precluded autonomy. I resigned, and subsequently accepted the position of Dean of Academic Affairs. God made a way, although I had presumed to run ahead of Him and had temporarily stepped out of His will for my life. I ascribe this success to God's favor over my life.

Chapter 7

Data Cleaning

Downstream Effects

Over the years I have found myself swimming against the tide. I learned the hard way that it is better to be in harmony with God—and most importantly, that to obey is better than sacrifice![xiv] When you are not enhancing your spirit, you make choices that harm yourself and run counter to intuition—you are in cognitive dissonance, and your life path becomes harmful. I decided that it was time to take a detour. I wanted to go straight to medical school after high school, but life threw me some curveballs. I was a little complacent in my last year of junior college, and my scores were not as competitive as they could have been. I applied to University of West Indies for the natural science program. I simultaneously applied to a pre-med program in New York, where my sister lived. I was accepted to a pre-med program at a college in New York.

I had only just begun to swim against the tide. I felt empowered and thought that I could achieve anything I put my mind to. I know from past experience that we can do exceedingly abundantly above all we can ask or think![xv] Most of all, I know that I am never alone. God's promises are true and perfect! I have learned over the years the value of forgiveness.[xvi] By faith, I have access to unlimited power!

Counterfactual Scenario

How I wish I could go back in a time machine and rewrite this part of the story—unfortunately, I do not get that luxury. As previously mentioned, I went to live with my older sister and this opportunity opened many doors for me. While waiting to pursue my medical education, I worked as a bank teller. I dated someone and ended up getting married at a very young age. The decision to get married subsequently thwarted my plans for medical school. I took a circuitous path that turned out to be providential, albeit punctuated with harsh realities. I am grateful for the lessons learned from this dark chapter in my life. I emerged stronger and more confident in myself. I was handed a package of heartbreak and disappointment, beautifully gift-wrapped with charm and deception.

Ultimate Betrayal

For years, I was haunted and tormented by a secret; I made a poor decision, a bad choice to keep a terrible secret for a friend. I was eating myself from the inside out; not quite hollow, but empty, because in my Christian upbringing I knew that what I had witnessed was wrong on many levels. Unfortunately, like other well-meaning Christians, I fell into the trap of stratifying sinful acts. Though well-intentioned, we are often guilty of assigning a hierarchy to sin—we ascribe a plethora of *degrees* to sins: big sins and little sins. I was so wrong! I chose to help a friend and then ended up losing the friendship anyway when, through a series of unfortunate circumstances, a thoughtless person betrayed my friend's confidence.

I have discovered over the years that when we remain silent instead of speaking out, we are *bullying* others. The ultimate betrayal is to yourself—being afraid to call out wrongdoing, standing complicit, using *moral licensing*, and compromising your values. We need to live intentionally. We should allow ourselves to become brave and vulnerable at the same time—our intention must inform our actions. Our goal should always be to stay open and loving and to reject mean-spiritedness.

Chapter 8
Life Study Protocol Deviations

Forgiveness

I have decided to live in forgiveness—that is the healthy choice. To forgive myself and to forgive others. According to a wise sage, "Unforgiveness is drinking poison and hoping it will kill your enemy" (Mandela n.d.). If we do not forgive others, how can we expect God to forgive us for our transgressions? I have moved on and forgiven the hurts, the abuse, the betrayals. The Bible also says, *"For I know the plans I have for you... plans to prosper you and not to harm you, plans to give you hope and a future."*[xvii] Forgiveness is liberating. I have forgiven myself for my bad choices, for betrayal, for being naïve and trusting, and for using truth as the default. I recognize that the human heart is desperately wicked, but I want to prosper and live in abundance. I choose to forgive and heal myself.

Answered Prayers

I was visiting a new church in a nearby county. This church was predominantly white, but I was told that there was a Jamaican gentleman there that I should meet. So, at the end of the service, I met this gentleman and we exchanged numbers. It turned out that he was from the same parish where I grew up in Jamaica, and he was acquainted with my parents and my brother. However, at that time, I had just emerged from a difficult divorce, and so I was not interested in any romantic relationships. So, I was oblivious to his advances, but he was persistent, and he was bold, and he swept me off my feet—and so here we are, twenty-seven years later!

Yes, in the spring of 1993, God gave me a second chance at love— after a whirlwind romance and a courtship lasting three months, I married my soulmate. Nine months later, my beautiful daughter,

Princess Alyssa, was born in 1994. Her birth was a testament to God's supernatural favor, as I had thought that I would never be a mother. Four years later, my beautiful *sumo wrestler,* Shane, was born. We affectionately called him a sumo wrestler because he was so big, he could not fit into his newborn baby clothes. My daughter literally prayed my son into existence. The moment I became pregnant, she announced that she had prayed for a brother. I quietly reminded her that we could not send the baby back if it turned out to be a girl. Thankfully, her prayer was answered just as she'd said!

Palpable Nostalgia

For years I was nostalgic—I paid the price for my bad decisions and poor choices; I had suffered because I lived so far away from my beloved siblings. Whenever my family visited me, the goodbyes were tough. I would dissolve into tears and cry unashamedly at airports, in the driveway, or wherever we chose to say our goodbyes. Consequently, when my daughter was born, I struggled with being far away from my family and lamented not having the network of support I craved. Of course, my mother visited me and stayed for a brief time. I made the tough decision to put my daughter in daycare when she was three months old. I had recently returned to the workforce after a series of company layoffs, mergers, and acquisitions.

Unexpected Findings

Tough Decisions

"If you have a difficult decision to make, do what is right!" (Twain n.d.) One day when I went to pick up my daughter from day care, I observed that *all eight bottles of formula* were untouched. I made the awful discovery despite numerous calls to check in on her during the day. The day care workers always assured me that she was doing fine. I was mortified and angry that she had not been fed all day! I promptly disenrolled her and quit my management job to take care of her. I have never regretted that decision. She is exceptionally bright and gifted—she was reading fluently before she turned two! Not surprising; *like mother like daughter,* as you will later see. Indeed, the apple doesn't fall from the tree!

Chapter 9

Strengths and Limitations

Perspectives on Leadership

The "Great Man" theory is flawed (Carlyle n.d.). Progressive scholars struggle to find consistency. I posit that leadership is earned; one is not born a leader. I have always been thrust into leading roles, whether by providence or by design, but not by choice. At seven years old, I was appointed secretary for my Sabbath school class, and thus, from an early age I had to address public audiences. Moreover, I was responsible for compiling the weekly minutes, and from this early age, I developed a healthy work ethic which has served me well all these years.

Return on Investments

We are truly the sum of all of our cumulative experiences, decisions, accomplishments, joys, disappointments, pains, and sorrows. Gerontologists refer to the phenomenon of being categorized in two or more vulnerable populations as *cumulative disadvantage,* so by virtue of being a black woman, my race and gender qualify me for the cumulative disadvantage status (Laub n.d.) (Sampson n.d.). Despite this dubious honor, I am proud to say: Look how far I've come! Yes, indeed—"Oh, the places you will go" (Seuss n.d.).

Indeed, it has been quite a journey, punctuated by speed bumps, potholes, triumphs, disappointments, pain, success—and, of course, failures. As the famous Negro spiritual says, "I wouldn't take nothin' for my journey now..." (Cesar n.d.). In fact, the more appropriate crescendo of my heart song would be: "If God didn't do anything else, He's already done enough!" (Crawford n.d.). Indeed, I proudly wear the mantle of survivor, mother, wife, sister, daughter, friend, cousin, mentor, professor, epidemiologist, gerontologist, nurse, and colleague, titles not ordered by sequence of importance.

Translating Research to Practice

Transition to Transcendence

A popular hymn says, "God moves in a mysterious way to perform his wonders" (William Cowper), and I agree. Through a series of circumstances, my son decided to spend his sophomore year commuting to school. He encountered some challenges during his freshman year, taking a gap year off afterward to realign his priorities and recalibrate some friendships. As a result of his commuting, we got to spend a lot of private time together catching up on lost time. I say this because sometimes I feel like I chose my career over him and neglected him in his critical senior year of high school.

Spirit and Letter of the Law

As Christians, sometimes we do not live the spirit of the law, we live the letter of the law. In ways, we are more legal than loving, and so I think my husband and I were rigid and inflexible in our parenting at times. For example, when my son wanted to play football, he would practice all week. Unfortunately, the games were usually on Friday nights after sunset, so we did not allow him to play since it was the Sabbath. This flip-flopping was creating cognitive dissonance for him, and he struggled. We all knew that Shane loved football, and we forced him to choose—we made mistakes as parents, but he forgave us for being inconsistent and imperfect parents. We did better as we knew better (Angelou n.d.).

Your Spotlight, Too

Upon reflection, I see that this is all muscle memory. I have always multi-tasked. Despite not gravitating to the spotlight, invariably I find myself center stage—while being a wife, mother, and full-time employee in middle-management, I successfully defended two theses and one dissertation. As an introvert, I do not like the spotlight.

However, I often find myself thrust into leadership roles or into the spotlight. I have grown to appreciate the strength of humility.

For example, I grappled with the decision to walk across the stage for my second master's degree, since I had already walked across the stage for my doctorate degree seven years earlier and had earned my first master's degree ten years earlier. Moreover, I wanted my daughter to enjoy her milestone. I did not want to eclipse her culmination of graduate school and subsequent celebration of a wonderful achievement as a graduate of a prestigious school of public health. I am glad I listened to my wise daughter. When the graduating committee learned that a mother and daughter would be graduating together, my daughter and I were contacted for an interview. In our interview with the *Emory Rollins School of Public Health Magazine,* my daughter reminded me, "Mom, it's your spotlight, too."

My high school peers had voted me "most likely to succeed," so they must have been clairvoyant. Though outwardly successful, I must confess that I used to be a coward. I recall running away from a playground fight that my bold older sister started—even though she knew she did not stand a chance against the class bully.

New Pathways

Fast-forward a couple of years—my son decided to move back home. He commuted to school, and that gave me the opportunity to spend a lot of time with him. He started going to a nearby park and began running in the middle of the day. At the time I was taking a sabbatical after leaving my job as program chair. I was starting to write my book. By the second week, I decided to put away whatever I was doing and go running with him. We became running buddies. As a result of that, I have changed my life physically and mentally. I am back in shape, and my son and I got to spend a lot of time together as we shared music and drove to the park where we ran three miles each day. Also, my daughter and I often carve out time from our busy schedules to practice yoga together.

Extrapolating the Data

Neurogenesis or Neuroplasticity

In moving from transition to transcendence, I have learned to guard my mind. Studies in neuroscience show that repeated thoughts become engraved into our minds with their own neurologic pathways. As a result of that, I am rewiring my mind, and I am increasing my neurogenesis and neuroplasticity (Bergland 2017). I am a better person. I am more intentional and deliberate in my thought patterns—accepting that not all thoughts passing through my mind every second are true.

Guard Your Mind

Further, I realize that not all of my perceptions are reality. Not all negative thoughts I used think about myself or others are true. I realize that I don't always have complete information, so I can't judge people. I can't always discern their motives. Only God can do that! I am intentional about walking into my abundance and claiming God's promises for my life. I know that God's love is intentional towards me, so I never doubt God. I trust Him implicitly, and that eliminates fear, anxiety, and doubt. The Bible states that perfect love casts out all fear![xviii] I trust the God who has given me peace to be a complete human being physically, mentally, spiritually, socially, and emotionally. I have incorporated physical lifestyle habits that improve my mind, thoughts, feelings, attitudes, and beliefs.

Recalibrating

I now refuse to take the work stresses home; I realize that too much stress keeps me from my purpose and causes me to lose focus, lose sleep, and neglect my healthy choices in diet and exercise. I fix my thoughts and my sleep patterns, as I realize that too much sugar neutralizes thiamine and B-vitamins, which are necessary to nourish my brain. I am making baby steps to improve my life as I fill my mind with positive thoughts. The Bible tells us to think thoughts that are true, honest, just, lovely, and of good report, which create excellence and support my authentic self.[xix] Moreover, I know that all things work together *for my good*![xx]

I am reconnecting with my authentic self, healing myself by setting healthy boundaries. Leo Tolstoy talks about "How much land does a dead man need?" and aptly answers, "Six feet!" so we shouldn't just be pursuing material and temporal things. I walked away from a six-figure income that was sucking the life out of me—I am developing and growing my best self and eliminating the stress and multitasking. I have stopped moving at a frantic pace just to please and support everyone else at the expense of myself. I choose to be happy!

Chapter 10

Generalization

Kaleidoscope

Indeed, everything is always working out for me, even if I do not see that at the time! I want to live a life of substance, knowing that it's very important how I touch other people's lives, and cognizant of Newton's third law of motion which states that "for every action there's an equal and opposite reaction" (Newton n.d.).

I can only control myself, not others. So, I am transforming my life to find my true purpose. My goal is to inspire everyone my life touches. I am living in awareness, knowing that there are always subtle whispers from the universe and that I must be attentive to God's still, small voice speaking to me. Life is all about growth and change, and so I have learned to be attentive and responsive to the subtle, divine promptings to find my purpose, knowing that God whispers to me; I can't fulfill my purpose and reach my full potential without being my authentic self.

Desiderata

GO PLACIDLY amid the noise and the haste,
and remember what peace there may be in silence.
As far as possible, without surrender, be on good terms with all persons.
Speak your truth quietly and clearly; and listen to others, even to the dull and the ignorant; they too have their story.
Avoid loud and aggressive persons; they are vexatious to the spirit. If you compare yourself with others, you may become vain or bitter, for always there will be greater and lesser persons than yourself.
Enjoy your achievements as well as your plans. Keep interested

in your own career, however humble; it is a real possession in the changing fortunes of time.

Exercise caution in your business affairs, for the world is full of trickery. But let this not blind you to what virtue there is; many persons strive for high ideals, and everywhere life is full of heroism.

Be yourself. Especially do not feign affection. Neither be cynical about love; for in the face of all aridity and disenchantment, it is as perennial as the grass.

Take kindly the counsel of the years, gracefully surrendering the things of youth.

Nurture strength of spirit to shield you in sudden misfortune. But do not distress yourself with dark imaginings. Many fears are born of fatigue and loneliness.

Beyond a wholesome discipline, be gentle with yourself.

You are a child of the universe no less than the trees and the stars; you have a right to be here.[xxi]

And whether or not it is clear to you, no doubt the universe is unfolding as it should.

Therefore, be at peace with God, whatever you conceive Him to be.

And whatever your labors and aspirations, in the noisy confusion of life, keep peace in your soul.

With all its sham, drudgery and broken dreams, it is still a beautiful world. Be cheerful. Strive to be happy.

(Ehrmann n.d.)

Child of the Universe

One of my siblings, a spiritual leader and close confidant to my mother, shared with me that Mom had a miscarriage before she became pregnant with me. My other sibling informed me that Mom bitterly grieved that miscarriage. Consequently, my older siblings tell me that Mom was very protective of me. She wanted me to be here. I could have been the baby she miscarried. God spared me for a purpose.

Notwithstanding, one of my older sisters felt that I was a spoiled brat, and so every chance she got she meted out cruel and unusual punishment to me. I was always hiding her novels or pranking her, so she got even with me when my mother was not looking!

For example, I would be in our front yard gardens skipping like Mr. Rogers, singing "It's a beautiful day in the neighborhood," only to be rudely awakened by a slipper or sandal flying in my direction, or being punished by one of my older sisters, who thought Mom was not punishing me enough for my *perceived* laziness. This was surely not the case, as everyone knows that my mother was the classic virtuous woman.[xxii] Of course, I valiantly defended myself by returning the favor or pranking my sister when she least expected it.

Non-modifiable Data

Not Here by Chance

I know that I am here by divine providence, not by accident. I look at the trajectory of my life and I am amazed at my life. How I have grown and changed over the years! Yet, God's goodness has stayed with me. My circumstances may have changed over the years, but I am using a lot of granularity to find my authentic self and to embrace my authentic power by God's grace!

I stand in awe of God's omnipresence and omnipotence in my life! Over the course of my life, all events have unfolded by pre-determination—God has led me perfectly![xxiii] As the songwriter shares (Crosby n.d.), "All the way my Savior leads me/What have I to ask beside?/Can I doubt His tender mercy/Who through life has been my guide?/...Though my weary steps may falter/And my soul athirst may be/Gushing from the rock before me/Lo a spring of joy I see!"

Part 3

Life Course Theory

Chapter 11
Statistical Findings

Love Story

A love story spanning sixty-five years—Arthur loved his Mable! Arthur chased Mable, a phenomenal, strong, proud woman, the second of five daughters born to Matilda and Gilbert Thomas. My maternal grandfather emigrated from Panama. He died before I was born, but his legacy lived on in my grandmother, his wife, whom we affectionately called Dottie. She was a force to be reckoned with. She was quick and witty and was always pristinely dressed. She had unparalleled culinary skills and was very sophisticated and wise. Before I knew what Spanish was, I recall her interspersing her communication with idiomatic expressions including *"Ven acá!"* which means, "Come here!"

My parents came from humble beginnings—my mom was a vibrant, strong, quiet, loving, compassionate house maker, dress maker, financial wizard, and cook. My father was an entrepreneur, contractor, and mason by trade who "never suffered fools lightly."

I had a rich heritage, as I grew up in a nurturing community with many cousins and aunts and my grandmother. I only knew one grandmother, as my other grandparents had died before I was born.

Reflections of Mom

Undoubtedly, Mom was the epitome of the virtuous woman. [xxiv] She was principled, had great wisdom and integrity, and was a dedicated, loving wife and mother. A rock and an anchor, she would pray for everyone. She instilled the values of hard work, honesty, and independence in each of us. Most of all, she was a prayer warrior. My older sisters would share that Mom possessed great athletic skills, as she would ride her bicycle in and around the community, over bridges, around sharp corners, and on the rough roads at speeds that defied gravity.

She was also an advocate for those who were less fortunate or disenfranchised. She always spread her wings to explore opportunities to advance herself. She was a strict disciplinarian, and my brothers would tell stories that even when they were in their teenage years and towered over Mom, she still had the ability to make them crumble and shrink as she disciplined them. She had the memory of an elephant and would not always immediately dispense punishment when an atrocity occurred.

She often delayed punishment, and when my brothers least expected it, she waited up late to administer punishment. When we had fevers, she massaged us with herbal concoctions and gave us teas to drink. As teenagers, my sisters and I recall that Mom often gave us gin and brandy when we were suffering from menstrual cramps. I remember her quiet strength as she imparted important values to us as children. The lessons and instruction have shaped our lives tremendously.

Praying Mother

I could always count on Mom to pray for me. She loved each of us uniquely, completely, and unselfishly. She showed me how to worship, how to make time for my family, how to prioritize. Mom taught me how to love reading the Bible to those who were unable to read for themselves. She loved to dance, and she would grab me as a young girl, twirling and spinning me until there was a big smile on my face. I could always count on Mom to pray for me, to lift my spirits, and to encourage me to aim for the stars.

She taught me how to share—she was thoughtful and generous in so many, countless ways. She inspired gratitude and thankfulness. She always said thank you, regardless of how small the kindness shown to her. In fact, her life was a symphony of gratitude. She displayed a thankful, happy spirit and never complained about any infirmities or injustices, real or perceived. She had such a tenacity for life. She loved unconditionally—words are inadequate to capture all that embodied her. She was the epitome of grace and strength. She loved Jesus. She was truly a phenomenal woman for whom I was grateful, and whom I am proud to call my mother.

According to my brothers, Mom had a smile that would disarm anyone. She was the consummate professional and knew how to multitask. She embodied the characteristics of the virtuous woman, and she would rise before daybreak to pray; she was ever on her knees interceding for all her family, friends, and even strangers. She could be compared to David, the man chasing after God's heart![xxv]

According to my little big sister, who towers over me physically and professionally, Mom modeled the best practice for worship. She was very protective of her children; she kept them on a short leash. She was a community service worker. She rescued many abused children, women, and animals. She was a prayer warrior and counselor. She loved to travel.

Mom instilled in her children a spirit of service and volunteerism. That legacy of service governs my life and my siblings' lives. My siblings have dedicated countless hours to taking care of the less fortunate and serving others in their spheres of influence. Similarly, my children and I have spent countless hours visiting elders at nursing homes and making dreams come true for elders or wards of the state. When my children were younger, my son played his saxophone for elders while my daughter played her violin for them. For many years, our family ritual on Christmas morning was to take gifts to residents of nursing homes and assisted living communities. We also participate in feeding the homeless and other community service events, as my mother used to do.

Mom was a phenomenal woman who shared her love for all. She was indisputably one of the most important people in our lives. She raised her thirteen children and was a mother figure to countless others. She displayed impeccable leadership skills; she led with humility, integrity, wisdom, and kindness. According to one family member, Mom "created a tapestry filled with wisdom and challenged us to serve, love, lead, and give each other guidance, caring, wisdom, and love." According to my niece, Mom had a steely strength and loved to sing with a beautiful soprano voice.

Chapter 12

Testimony of My Father

Dad loved God, his wife, his children, his grandchildren, animals, and the less fortunate. He encouraged us to get a sound education and to strive for the best. My father was a very brave, fearless, and caring man. He was very proud of his children, and he would repeat stories of their high school experiences in his later years. He demanded respect for the elders. He would do masonry work, farming, contracting, and animal husbandry. He was a skilled marksman.

Dad had a beautiful tenor voice. He was very active in church and community service. He did all in his power to meet the needs of his church family and friends. Every chance he got, he would talk about Christianity, and he guarded the Sabbath with tenacity. He loved to interact with neighbors and was quite the gregarious person. My father was a passionate, strong, caring, and generous man—he would give you the shirt off his back, so much so that we as children were concerned that people took advantage of his kindness; he loved the church. He spent his life in service to the church and community. However, he didn't suffer fools gladly. He was a man with a purpose, a man on a mission, and respected one's time. I remember, growing up, that he was always on time—if we were late for any events he would drive away, and we had to find our own way there.

Altruism Personified

He was concerned for those less fortunate than himself, even when he was sick and unable to move around. He was still an advocate for the weak and those in need. My father was the champion of the underserved. I recall that when I was little and almost severed my tongue, my father took me to the hospital and the doctor had to give me stitches. I remember how he argued with the doctor and nurses because they didn't give me any local anesthesia. He was my protector and advocate. Like David, the Psalmist,[xxvi] he was a man after God's heart. He was also a strong proponent of not touching the Lord's anointed and doing them no harm![xxvii] He was a gentleman, a provider, and a family man with a heart of gold. Despite his short stature, he was indeed a giant among men; he loved his children, and he was very present in our lives. His face would light up when we entered the room, and he made each of us feel special, although everyone knew I was his favorite!

My father valued and respected everyone. In particular, he taught us to respect each other, especially our elders. One day, he walked in as I was talking back to my big sister, who had assigned me a chore which I did not want to do. Dad inquired if I was talking to my older sister in such a disrespectful tone. He then proceeded to give me the *only* spanking I ever received from him.

Dad was always supportive and encouraging of my academic pursuits. I remember after representing my high school in the National School's Challenge Bowl, he was the first person to meet me when I returned home from the event. He was so proud of me—I will always treasure the times I spent with my dad. He loved to tell stories, and you could sit for hours and listen to him. He was consistently inconsistent and perfectly imperfect!

Daily Study Protocol

Growing up, I recall feeling as though we were *sentenced* to family worship first thing in the morning and last thing at night. We couldn't watch television on Wednesday nights because according to my dad, it was prayer meeting night. Thus, on Wednesday nights, we either went to church or worshipped at home. My parents guarded the edges of the Sabbath.

I recall, however, one Sabbath morning I happened to wake up earlier than normal, and I saw Dad with his head glued to the radio, listening to a cricket match between the West Indies and Australia.

Being feisty, I questioned why he was listening to cricket on the Sabbath. To which he replied, "This is my house!"

My father was one of the hardest-working individuals I've known. The consummate entrepreneur, he had multiple streams of income—he seemed to work twice as hard as the average man because he had a large family. He was beyond generous and caring. He was a good steward of his resources and felt a responsibility to his church and home community.

Study Associations

My siblings... where do I begin?

My family was humongous because both of our parents had huge families, and so we had a plethora of cousins, nieces, and nephews. Strangely enough, I didn't have any uncles because my father's two older brothers had died at a young age, and my mother only had sisters. My family is a force to be reckoned with—never mess with one, because you must contend with multiple others! As a result of our parents being so active in church and the community, we had a massive extended family of church members and community supporters. We always knew that we were loved, respected, and supported. Our parents lived a life of substance, value-laden with the rich principles of respect for everyone and love for everyone. I truly enjoyed a rich childhood punctuated by community love and support. Indeed, it truly takes a village!

One of my older sisters had immigrated to the United States from early age; she demonstrated selfless love and unconditional support for her siblings. I remember during the high school years she would send us the most beautiful, fashionable outfits with matching shoes. She is beautiful and has the prettiest legs of all the girls. An eternal optimist, she always saw the best in everyone but was not afraid to tell you the truth, whether you liked it or not. I owe her a debt of gratitude for rescuing me from a difficult situation.

Competing Priorities

One of my older sisters came to visit me in Queens, N.Y. I had dropped out of school, had my drapes pulled, and my home was dark and gloomy. I was disheveled and in the fetal position—she packed my clothes in her hatchback sportscar and told me she did not want to have to explain to our parents if anything happened to me. So, I moved in with her and she nurtured and supported me. She helped me find myself again. I will never forget her kindness. She's one of my favorite siblings and one of my best friends. She is selfless and will give you the shirt off her back!

We talk on a consistent basis and almost seem to know what each other is thinking. She loves family; she spends her time in community service, much like our mother did. She manages to care for the older ladies on her street whose family are not present in their lives. She is also a survivor. When the rest of my family immigrated to the United States, everyone landed at her home. She has no filter—she says what she means and means what she says. She is brutally honest.

Thank you for your kindness, thank you for your love and support to your siblings and your parents; thank you. I will never forget your thoughtfulness and generosity and how much your love and support meant to us over the years.

Exclusion Criteria

Taking the Puppies to the River

The story is told that some of my older siblings were tired of babysitting the younger siblings. Moreover, my parents rescued everything and everyone. The older boys were charged with making dog food, which consisted of cornmeal with leftovers. If the boys forgot to feed the dogs, my father would wake them up no matter how late it was. Sometimes in frustration they would not wait to cool the food, and the poor dogs would yelp when the hot food clung to their palate. My father would punish my brothers for mistreating the dogs. On another occasion, I am told that a few of my older siblings were annoyed with all of the rescued dogs and proceeded to abandon a new litter of dogs at the river. When my father discovered this heinous act, he went looking for the puppies by the riverside. The siblings suffered the consequences of this thoughtless act!

Sneaking Off to Athletic Championships (CHAMPS) Instead of Going to Church

We were not allowed to attend secular events on the Sabbath, so my older sister would pretend we were going to church and ended up taking us to national sports events, much to the chagrin of my parents. We were not allowed to wear so-called men's attire, so we would hide jeans in the trunk of the car. Once the car disappeared from my parents' view, we would stop the car and change our clothes to the more appropriate attire.

Chapter 13
Inclusion Criteria

Career Trajectory

As a result of my invincible optimism and innate drive for success, I increased a nursing program pass rate from 52% to 77.4 % in nine months. I persevered; I impatiently climbed the rough side of the career mountain. Subsequently, I have inspired positive change for many students, mentored transitioning graduates, and developed faculty. When my season ended, I moved to my next chapters.

Ivory Towers

As a black woman, I successfully navigated the ivory towers of academia, "a place where dreams go to die." I confronted the overt white privilege, pervasive institutionalized racism, and palpable discrimination. Although not clear to me at the time, the Bible says that "all things work together for good"![xxviii] Although not seeing the rainbow at the time, I wondered when I would reap the rewards of my hard work. I later discovered that in every instance of unfair treatment, I was vindicated.

As one enemy's attacks were thwarted, legions rose in their place. It often became the norm that despite my strong research acumen and invaluable contributions to research enterprise, my hard work was not valued or rewarded. I often felt blacklisted. In a few notable instances, although I was integral in the recruitment of study participants and reviving failing studies, I was often omitted from publications when I transferred from one principal investigator to another, based on funding changes and re-organizations of labs. Nevertheless, in one year, I collaborated with my peers and mentors and was instrumental in producing seven abstracts. The abstracts were accepted for publication, and some findings have been presented at national and international conferences. To God be the glory!

Job Survival Analysis

Job Survival Curves

I refused to quit or walk away quietly into the darkness. I rose buoyantly with the buffering power of incredible and unseen force. I rose with eagle's wings. I always knew that God had a plan for my life; I knew that I could turn lemons into lemonade. I always perceived myself as a winner; I survived abusive relationships. The goal of my story is not to create sensationalism; I am a very private person. My story is a testimony to the fighting spirit, resilience, and unwavering faith in God. I am not a victim; I am a victor! I am humbled and honored about all the places one can go when one has unwavering faith and trust in God, who has promised to take us the distance!

I am the girl with the extra digits who was temporarily broken, and I reinvented myself like the phoenix. I rose from the ashes, turned rubble into noble. I used my enterprising spirit of resilience and broke free—free to assume my rightful place from unusual to extraordinary, as I pursued a destiny of non-negotiable faith undergirding my spirit of relentless perseverance. I encountered many angels along the way. I discovered the kindness of strangers and mentors.

God prompted me to write my story, not about sensationalism, but about showing others that they can overcome adversity and rise triumphant. My story is one of brokenness, betrayal, and bravery. I was born blessed with extra digits, which have since been surgically removed. Hence, my family always felt that I was gifted and destined for greatness. I believe that my story is one of inspiration about triumph over personal trials and a testimony to determination, faith, and resilience. With hard work, we can accomplish anything!

Backward Regression Analysis
Begin with the End in Mind

One of my favorite authors admonishes us to "begin with the end in mind," in the renowned *7 Habits of Highly Effective People* (Covey n.d.), so I will tell you what I hope to accomplish by sharing my story with each of you. I recently walked away from a six-figure executive position in pursuit of inner peace and to fulfill my purpose of inspiring others to dream big. I would like to share my story with others—as a result of my dedication, hard work, and quest for excellence, I was able to transform a failing national nursing program to a point of stability and trending upwards.

I embrace my story of struggle and triumph as I conquered a cardiovascular anomaly which should have resulted in being on lifetime medication, survived two abusive relationships, overcame rape and bankruptcy, and navigated academia using unwavering faith to arrive at my destination of triumph, miracles, and victory.

Ye of Little Faith

I share the negative, the positive, the gore and the glory, the victimization, and the victory. I never thought I could have children, but today I have two beautiful, well-adjusted young adults. I have been married for twenty-seven years to my soulmate and the love of my life.

My naysayers thought I was crazy—I walked away from a perceived lucrative and influential job. I was inspired to go on a three-month sabbatical. As a fluke, I decided to realign my career priorities. I removed myself from a toxic environment—I wanted a healthy space to grow and develop.

I know that it was by divine providence that I flipped to YouTube, and once I encountered a certain motivational speaker, I got the confirmation—I was inspired to write my story. As a result of my education, experience, training, and unwavering faith in God, I have come this far. I would like to share with others that nothing is impossible; with hard work and prayer, we can truly conquer all!

I stay grounded with all that embodies my life. This story is an act of courage as I confront my past demons and fears, and embrace my triumphs. I deserve to be here in this space and time. I never forget that actions have consequences, and I know that we are all accountable for our actions. Most of all, I refuse to allow anyone to define or limit me. I do not seek permission from anyone. I own my seat at the table. I deserve to be here. I have paid my dues; this is my time. I boldly approach the throne of grace and reach out for all that God has for me.

I know that God is the source of all good things, and He is in control![xxix] In partnership with God, we are the arbiters of our success. Never forgetting that we have the awesome responsibility to share, inspire, and touch lives, and to inspire positive change with unquestionable ethics. Being cognizant of obligations that accompany responsibilities—the necessity of developing moral characters and keeping that compass pointed to the True North. I must reiterate: the sky is the limit.

I glide onto the runway—I welcome this moment of destiny with open arms. I enter this place of safety, fulfilment, and restoration. Indeed, the stars are aligned! Destiny was delayed, but not denied!

Chapter 14

Preliminary Data

It's Not Just Finding My Destiny—It's About My Journey of Faith

I have come to embrace the patterns, contours, detours, and trajectories of my life. I embrace its purpose, victories, disappointments, and crossroads. Knowing that my past informs and forms me; knowing that each encounter and experience sculpts my essence and permeates my being. I now appreciate every obstacle and opportunity.

I massaged the "book idea" for years but could not slow down enough to begin this project—competing priorities burgeoned year after year. I seemed to pursue one dead-end opportunity after the other. I took the risk of chasing elusive academic dreams; I dared greatly! (B. Brown 2013). After much deliberation, I reluctantly put this project on hold. I have been waiting for the right moment in time. God has a way of reminding us that without faith it is impossible to please Him,[xxx] and He dictates the seasons of our lives.

In a brilliant splash of clarity, I dared to make a move which would change my life in unimaginable ways. In a moment that seemed ethereal, I shocked everyone by resigning from my *presumed* influential job. I was Chief Nursing Administrator, and my academic presence with accrediting agencies and licensure bodies was impressive. For all intents and purposes, I had accomplished my American dream, all these years later, after my unceremonious arrival in New York.

Unbeknownst to everyone, in my private moments I was restless, unchallenged, and desperately unhappy. I grew professionally stagnant. I allowed myself to be bullied. I was underappreciated, and tolerated, *not celebrated,* for my forward planning and foresight in creating ambitious programs—programs which were later adopted and implemented at my departure. Unsurprisingly, others received the credit for my successful and bold initiatives. I was tired of trying to please everyone, because I know that is an exercise in futility.

I felt pulled in a million directions. The ivory tower demands were grueling and stifling. I felt bullied by senior leadership. I could not derive energy from my leadership team, who were grossly inept and unprepared for the job. The organization chart was skewed. I was in a state of cognitive dissonance all the time. I was reminded that our wants are not always the wants of the stakeholders—we must think of our wants and the sensory data we are trying to convey.

I love the way one evangelist articulates that "if the request is wrong, God says 'no'; if the timing is wrong, God says 'slow'; if you need fixing, God says 'grow'; and if the timing is right, the request is right, and you are right, God says 'go!'" (Jeremiah n.d.).

So, what is the story I am trying to tell? I'm trying to say that nothing is impossible! Especially when you construct your life course on a rich, solid foundation of integrity, humility, ethics, endless Christian love, and childlike faith. Nurturing the spirit of gratitude and contentment with your circumstances, knowing that for everything, there is a season. Put God first, and be confident that He will take care of the rest.

Chapter 15

Study Attrition

Suffering Illness and Loss

Sometimes good people suffer, and we don't understand why. I remember my mom who, despite being such a beautiful person inside and out, despite being a community service worker, and despite exemplifying charity to those in need, really suffered at the end of her life.

For several years prior to her death, Mom experienced a lot of transient ischemic attacks (TIAs). My family recalls how the TIAs occurred without warning—she would literally be in a serious conversation with someone, and without warning she would seem to disappear within herself and become frozen, like in a trance. These episodes appeared to be painless, and she would snap out of them pretty quickly. There were no apparent cognitive or neurological deficits or residual effects that we could see with the naked eye, but I think, as research suggests, that they were leading up to the big one!

In the end, Mom had a massive heart attack, which was really debilitating. The physicians were amazed that she survived, but she was never the same afterward. I remember taking six weeks off from my job to go and take care of her, and being the meticulous, overprotective daughter, I detested the caregiver's work ethics and lack of compassion. My frustration was the cause of discord and discontent with my siblings, who thought a certain caregiver was doing a great job. As a matter of fact, Mom went through a lot of caregivers, because some were just there for the paycheck; they didn't really care about her or love the job.

I think one caregiver was not as caring as I would have liked! My dad agreed—he thought she was abusive to my mom and very pretentious. Whenever anyone else was around, she did a great show about how much she loved Mom. She deserved an Oscar for her professed undying love for my Mom. I saw right through her. I saw how disingenuous she was; she was rough. But I have forgiven her—they saying hurting people are sometimes unintentionally hurtful.

Anyway, I spent beautiful moments singing songs and reading the Bible with my mom, and just talking with her and encouraging her. She seemed to enjoy simple acts, like foot massages. I enjoyed letting her know how much she was loved and cared for. I know she suffered in the end—sometimes the pain was so bad she just said grimaced and closed her eyes and whispered, "Jesus! Jesus! Yes, Lord!"

She really suffered. I am glad the Lord called her home, because there is no quality-of-life or dignity once you can no longer perform your activities of daily living. Mom resigned herself to the new status quo—albeit reluctantly. She lost her dignity, and being such a proud woman, that did not sit well with her, and then she died. I know one day if I am faithful, I will see her again.

In a similar way, Dad suffered bad health in the end. He always had circulation problems, hypertension, and cardiovascular issues. I remember soon after I became a new nurse, my dad went in for his annual colonoscopy, and the clinicians ruptured his colon. And then his health declined, and we all thought we had lost him for good. He gave up on life, and he became a shell of himself. I took time off from work to nurse him back to health. My sisters tell me they think my love and tender care turned him around. I take no credit and know that everything is in God's hands, and clearly, God wanted to give him more time to resolve any unresolved issues.

When the time was right, God took him home. I remember the last weekend before Dad passed. I spent time with him in the hospital, and he was at peace. I played all his favorite songs on my phone and sang with him—we had a prayer meeting. It was beautiful, and so I know my dad had made his calling and election sure! I will see him again in the world made new. As Seventh-day Adventists, we believe in the second coming of Jesus Christ, and so we believe there is a life after death.

Chapter 16

Epitome of Quiet Strength and Grace

I have come out of the empty spaces, the unhappy places—I have come into the light. I did not always see the horizon. I often detoured, deviated; the path was thorny and less traveled. God brought me back in alignment with His will for my life. I am truly blessed. God polished me and prepared me, albeit reluctantly at times. I can now claim my purpose and walk into my destiny. I am a woman of substance and a force to be reckoned with because of my non-negotiable faith.

At every step of my journey, I was propelled forward by a strength which was not always discernable. I could always look back to see the interwoven threads of faith or the variations on the theme of faithfulness. I believe in someone bigger than myself. I always knew that if I fell, I could get up. I knew that I could count on family, and that no matter what I did, I was loved and supported unconditionally.

There may have been detours and challenges, but I believe that God has been my rock and my fortress. I always felt the Lord's protection as I navigated unfriendly waters and dark shadows. God is my fortress, rock, and beacon in the storms of life. He has put a wall of fire around me. He has been the glory in my midst. The Bible says "I will put a wall of fire around her... I will be the glory in her midst"![xxxi] I always knew that God was there, looking after me. He was faithful in His promises to never leave me nor forsake me.

Admonition

Thus, my admonition is to "lean on the everlasting arms" and trust Jesus to work His purpose out in our lives. I obey God's promptings to forgive the unforgivable, love the unlovable, and to confidently turn every situation to His omnipotence! Love boldly and aim for the stars. With prayer and hard work, you can accomplish your dreams and exceed your wildest expectations. I chased my destiny relentlessly; a destiny which has been elusive at times. I had to be uncomfortable with my *status quo* and willing to move into unforeseen paths and walk the road less traveled.

I often ventured out onto unfamiliar paths and ended up overcorrecting multiple times. I often compensated for the shortcomings and missed opportunities. I chased my destiny but undoubtedly found the joy-centered life, punctuated by non-negotiable faith. I have loved all of me. All the negative yet rich experiences have made me who I am. I always knew I could achieve unsurmountable goals; I relished the rich experiences, because my faith undergirded everything I did. Indeed, it has been one incredible journey, but like the songwriter (Cesar n.d.) says, "I wouldn't take nothin' for my journey now." Thank you, God, the author and finisher of my faith!

Chapter 17

Identifying Themes

I remember interviewing for a staff nurse position at a leading southeastern hospital while I worked on my doctorate. I just wanted a position with no leadership responsibilities so I could focus on my dissertation. Once the hiring manager perused my curriculum vitae (CV), she immediately elevated me to a supervisory role. I remember showing up to this job one Monday morning to assume the unit leader position. Unbeknownst to me, HR had failed to inform the unit of my arrival. No one was expecting me; no announcements were disseminated to the nursing units. Unfortunately, as I have learned too well over the years, nurses are a peculiar "species" who have been known to "eat their young," and my tepid welcome testified to this idiom!

Nurses who presumed they were next in line for the promotion to the new leadership role were not happy that the company had decided to go outside of the organization to hire me—having a certain prestigious university in my pedigree added fuel to this fire of discontent and disgruntlement. My background created tension among the leadership team and resulted in more frustration among teams on the medical-surgical unit.

Study Amendments

I had my late adapters; I had people from day one who drew battle lines. However, being a strong, brave, phenomenal Black woman with presumed *Ashanti* blood in her veins, I did not back away from the challenge. Curiously, as unit manager, I found it challenging to become acclimated to a culture where leadership was akin to a figurehead with no autonomy and a lack of resources. In fact, more often than not, I was penalized for my incumbents' medical errors—whenever a staff member made a mistake, I discovered that I was suspended along with the culprit. Within a year of assuming the role, I bristled at the incongruence with my values and decided that this was not the role for me. I took the opportunity to learn and grow from this strange experience. The apostle Paul said it best about fighting the good fight.[xxxii]

Confirmatory Processes

When I worked as a nurse-extern for another large hospital, I realized that nurses were expected to be docile, subservient, and submissive. As a psychology major and business executive with nursing as second career, I realized that this job constantly threw me into a state of *cognitive dissonance.* I remembered being in previous roles where I was the only female and the only person of color in the boardroom—I was not expected to speak up or advocate for the underserved or marginalized. In fact, one manager had the effrontery to caution me to "just listen and not say anything."

I refused to be limited and defined by others—so unlike my nursing peers, and much to the chagrin of my unit director, I spoke up to physicians, challenged long-held beliefs and assumptions, and inspired and advocated for colleagues. I knew that I could be assertive and respectful and still do a good job. Unfortunately, I was perceived as a "maverick," so this job did not last very long.

Part 4
Reclaiming My Destiny

Chapter 18
Spurious Findings

Destiny Delayed, Not Denied

"I don't think you're going to make it! Karen, can I speak with you for a moment? I'm really worried about you." I bristled at my professor's words. Momentarily, I felt like I could not breathe. I was surprised, disappointed, and hurt all at the same time. The assertion was even more painful because the professor happened to be someone whom I admired and wanted to emulate. I am not angry with her. She revealed her human nature. Like so many of us, she was operating with incomplete information. I immediately shared with her that I was commuting over sixty miles, one way, to the clinical site while concurrently working on my master's degree in gerontology, along with my accelerated BSN program. She remarked that I may have bitten off more than I could chew. I knew differently.

How many times do educators make spurious conclusions about student's futures when they make assumptions and operate with incomplete information? God has the final say! The professor's prediction that I would not aspire to my dream of being a nurse was not surprising, because she did not know the backstory. It is true that invariably I would show up to my clinical sites late. This is because I lived almost sixty miles from the clinical site to which I was thoughtlessly assigned. I remember thinking how shortsighted the clinical coordinator was. She failed to assign students close to their homes—in another rotation I traveled ninety miles to a clinical site.

As a result of the warped clinical placement, I had to wake up early and leave my home by 5:00 a.m. for my clinical rotations. However, like clockwork, it rained every single day I went to the clinical site. Not just a little rain, but torrential downpours, during which visibility was dangerously impaired. Every morning as I traveled down the single-lane highways to the clinical site, I gripped the steering wheel with fear and anxiety. My visibility was reduced to less than half a mile. I could barely see as the wipers struggled in vain to keep the rain off the wind screen. I remember praying to Jesus, "Lord, help me; Lord, have mercy; Jesus, keep me safe." In hindsight, I see how my judgment was warped because sometimes I would subconsciously close my eyes and let go of the steering wheel. I know it is nothing short of a miracle that I am here to write my story.

Competing with Mother Nature

I will repeat for emphasis: Like clockwork, every single clinical day, it rained buckets. The thunderstorms assailed me. So, I would arrive at the clinical sites late because I could barely drive more than five miles an hour, even though I left my house more than two hours in advance to get to the site. I would arrive late and be flustered because I knew that tardiness was non-negotiable, but I was just thankful to be alive. When my professor remarked that she didn't think I would make it, I could see where she was coming from. If she only knew what I went through to get to the clinical site, every single day of the six-week clinical rotation.

Clearing the Hurdles

If only my professor knew the hurdles I cleared just to get to class. I had a ninety-minute commute, on a good traffic day! Sometimes I would drive to college and not have enough gas. I remember unceremoniously using quarters to pay for gas and praying that there was enough in the tank to get me back and forth from school.

I recall enrolling for courses not knowing where tuition was coming from. Coming from Jamaica, with my pre-conceived ideas about independence and prideful living, I thought that financial aid was an extension of welfare, so I often worked during the day to pay my way through school. One day my classmate remarked that she had a refund from student loans. She then gave me a quick lecture on financial aid, so afterwards I promptly applied for financial aid!

I was always good with numbers, and my years working in the banking industry paid off and proved fortuitous. I discovered that if I enrolled in more than twelve credits, the tuition was the same as twelve credits. I quickly sought overrides, and so it was not unusual for me take eighteen or twenty-two credits per semester. Consequently, I finished my first four-year degree (a BS in psychology) in three years and my second accelerated (BSN) undergraduate degree in less than eighteen months. Talk about a return on investment!

God Winks

I could see God "wink" (Rushnell n.d.) throughout my education and career trajectory. I am convinced that God has a sense of humor, because despite my professor's prognostication I am the *only student* over the last thirteen years, from any nursing cohort, to go on to receive two masters' degrees, as well as a PhD in nursing. I was also offered a post-doctoral fellowship from a prestigious research university. Oh, the places I have gone!

Second Career

Nursing became a second career for me. I had previously worked successfully in finance and strategic management for over thirteen years. I experienced my share of acquisitions, company relocations, and downsizings. The instability was frightening. My former boss, as well as my sisters, encouraged me to enroll in nursing courses. Initially I had bristled at the suggestion, because my lifelong dream was to be a physician. In certain socializations, nursing was once considered "settling," especially for someone like me who had supposedly done well in my previous academic pursuits. For many years I had subconsciously subscribed to the false narrative that some professions were more "noble" than others.

Quiet Crucible

One writer talks about the anonymous years when we feel abandoned. In my "quiet crucible" (Chole n.d.), God gave me a beautiful picture. He has really worked on me over the years, so now I remind myself that self-control is indeed a *fruit of the Spirit*. Self-control not only means to be in control of your appetite, but also of your emotions and your decisions (Chole n.d.). Successful leaders master their emotions! Consequently, I have learned to manage the way I feel and to operate in a spirit of transparency and vulnerability, all the while being cognizant of the impact of my thoughts, feelings, attitudes, and beliefs, because I have discovered that once you say the words you cannot un-ring the bell; you cannot put the toothpaste back in the tube; once you put it out into the atmosphere, it's going to manifest itself in ways consistent with the law of attraction. We know that for every action, there is an equal and opposite reaction (Newton n.d.).

Chapter 19

Threats to Study Validity

Confounding Data

My advice to young women is to avoid compromising friendships—if something feels wrong, then it is wrong. At twenty-five years old, I was naïve, gullible, and chasing my demons. I sometimes made poor decisions. Decisions have consequences. I made the wrong choice to be friends with the wrong person. This decision almost cost me my life. This person verbally, physically, and psychologically abused me. I was so trusting! This person surreptitiously bugged my phone and violated me in many ways. I naively allowed myself to be taken advantage of; this person took advantage of my friendship. I was mistreated by someone who claimed to love me and wanted to make further advances, which I rebuffed, and who resorted to maligning my character.

Contaminated Data

I am by no means a victim. I say all this to provide context to where the Lord has brought me from. Abuse comes in many forms, sizes, and shapes. The Lord has protected and cared for me. I remember someone pointing a long knife at me and threatening me. God saved me! I recall being told that someone had a loaded gun and could hurt me. God saved me!

One night when my mom was visiting me, someone whom I considered a friend tried to take advantage of me. I felt that my life was in danger, because this individual began stalking me. On one occasion, he tried to run me over with his car as he told me, "If I can't have you, no one else can have you." Again, God saved me!

Retrospective Data

Nothing is impossible with God! God has the final say—it's not over until God says it's over. The disappointments, the roadblocks, the stumbling blocks, the mistakes, the missteps, the failures, and the pains are all temporary setbacks. We're all a part of a master plan, with God orchestrating everything behind the scenes to bring us to a perfect end.

Motivation doesn't have an expiration date. Setbacks are setups for comebacks. I have learned to master my circumstances and to not be a prisoner to my past. I've learned to embrace *all of me*—the ugly, the good, the bad, the negatives, and the positives—because they all make me who I am today.

I've learned not to let people limit or define me. I've learned that I give people permission to treat me the way they do. I have learned to press on towards the mark of the high calling of God in Christ. Like Paul, I can say that I have fought the good fight and finished the course and pray for God to enlarge my territory.[xxxiii] I am no longer chasing my destiny. I am aligning my dreams and my plans with the master plan, with the Creator, the One who is my source, the One who put the stars in place, the One who knows me by name and numbers all the hairs on my head.

The One who said He has a plan for me to give me hope and a future! Like the apostle Paul, I keep pressing forward to the mark of the high calling![xxxiv] I have been humbled and polished like a diamond in the rough. I've been groomed and made more transparent, more formidable, more human. Arrogance and ego have no place in my life. I dare greatly!

Chapter 20
Generativity

New Beginnings

I endorse the saying that I'm not a prisoner of my past, but I'm a product of what my future has become through Christ. I freely embrace my failures and my achievements. I boast in God's goodness—I'm not a product of my past, but a promise for my future! I live my life consistent with the lyrics of the old hymn: "I'm pressing on the upward way/New heights I'm gaining every day/...Lord, plant my feet on higher ground." (Johnson Oatman n.d.) Moreover, the Bible tells us to be content, no matter what circumstances we find ourselves in.[xxxv]

God is my peace, my joy, He will never leave me or abuse me; He is my redeemer, my comforter, my provider, my peace. When I am weak, He makes me strong; when I'm lost, He's my compass. He shows me the way. We are told to be strong and courageous.[xxxvi] Joshua says to be strong and courageous, for the Lord our God is with us. We are told that eyes have not seen, nor ears heard all the marvelous things the Lord has in store for us people.[xxxvii] We press forward to all the marvelous things because Lord has promised us. Nothing is impossible with God![xxxviii]

Cutting My Losses

After my divorce, I experienced financial hardship from various obligations. I grieved the loss of a marriage, and my work and health suffered tremendously. I was unable to perform at work and my boss told me I was taking off too many sick days. I eventually lost my Fortune 500 job. Soon afterwards, I was diagnosed with a cardiovascular anomaly. I was supposed to be on lifetime medications. I remember being lonely and broke.

I remember one day, I was laying prostrate on the floor, crying, and praying to God to send me a friend. My big sister, the consummate prayer warrior, called and prayed with me that God would send me a friend. The very next day, I met the man who would change my life forever. We dated for three months and then got married. It has been twenty-seven years of trials and triumphs, but if I had to do it all over again, I would marry him, the love of my life, my soulmate! He is such a gentle and sweet person—roses and breakfast in bed are quite commonplace!

Tenacity

Destiny Chaser

After multiple company relocations, acquisitions, and mergers, my sisters impressed upon me the need to find a more stable career. I had taken time off to raise my young children. After much deliberation, and the prompting of my then-boss, I enrolled in nursing school. At that time, I worked at a large hospital where I coordinated a healthcare program. I had a bachelor's degree in psychology, so I was able to complete an accelerated nursing program in eighteen months. To God be the glory! I thank God for His supernatural favor and leading in my life. I am reminded that nothing is impossible when you put your trust in God.

In another instance, a recruiter contacted me and offered me a position that paid $20,000 more than my current position, and so I joined this "dot com" company which was preparing for Y2K. I joined this national company, where I was responsible for the accounting function for North America—a $10M portfolio. I travelled about thirty percent of the time. It was not uncommon for me to travel back and forth to California every few weeks. I also remember using "net meeting" technology that allowed me to stay in Atlanta and interview prospective employees in California. This was a "dot com" company, and the html technology was new and exciting. Not soon after I was recruited, the company was acquired in the era of mergers and acquisitions. Looking back, I can see that

God was orchestrating my future without my being aware of it. He has led me perfectly!

Academia—the Place Where Dreams Go to Die

There were dark times in academia, "the place where dreams go to die." For ten years, I struggled to get a job that was commensurate with my education, experience, and training. It was a wicked and dark time. I remember leaving work after an extremely difficult and challenging day that had pushed me to my limits. As I was walking down the stairs, my legs felt like lead with fatigue. I had the startling epiphany that Jesus *saw me*, saw my sufferings and desperation. I immediately felt enveloped in God's presence and felt His invisible arms encircling me. Once I knew that God was with me and looking at all the abuse, bullying, and unfair and unequal treatment, I found a semblance of peace amidst the chaos and confusion.

After my daughter matriculated to university, she was awarded a $200,000 courtesy scholarship. By virtue of my daughter's scholarship, an individual in a senior position verbalized, "You just received a $50,000 a year raise"—clearly, that blessing did not sit well with them. I felt thrust into spiritual warfare. This senior leader made an *overt*, concerted effort to remove me from my position. I actively pursued other positions, which never materialized. Although I consistently received stellar reviews and appraisals, I only received the typical three percent annual raise. I felt frustrated because my white counterparts were promoted to bigger positions, albeit with less experience and education. Soon I was part of a reduction in force due to *sequestration of research funding*, despite the fact that I was coordinating multi-million-dollar research projects. But God is faithful; He never gives us more than we can bear. He *grooms* and *polishes* us during the lean times; He prepares us for the future He has reserved for us. If we remain faithful, and trust God's leading, which is not always easy, we will ultimately emerge victorious.

Chapter 21

Spontaneous Misfiring

One day during that early first marriage, I had a very excruciating pain in my side and went to the doctor. The doctor informed me that I had an ectopic pregnancy, which spontaneously miscarried. I was disappointed, and afterwards tried unsuccessfully to become pregnant. I foolishly thought that a baby would save an unsalvageable marriage. Thank you, God, for closing that door! In hindsight, I see the blessing of those barren years—looking back now, I consider myself very lucky. I would not want a constant reminder of those awful years.

So, for many years, I thought I would never be a mother. I have relatives who have struggled with infertility, so I was resigned to exploring other options to create the family that I had always wanted. Imagine my pleasant surprise when, soon after marrying my soulmate, I discovered that I was pregnant. My daughter was conceived during our honeymoon. God can restore and give life to barren wombs. My son was born five years later. What a marvelous thing God has done—not one, but two babies! Ask and we will receive... seek and we will find, when we trust God![xxxix]

Making Bold Assertions

One day, I came to the realization that my first marriage was over. I found the name of a divorce attorney and drove over thirty miles for the consultation. After completing the paperwork, the attorney counselled me to think about the filing for twenty-four hours and then return to finalize the paperwork. Once the twenty-four hours had expired, and after much prayer and reflection, I got in my car and drove through rush hour traffic to the attorney's office. I arrived at the address where I thought the attorney's office was located. To my dismay, I realized that I was at the wrong place.

I drove around in circles for the better part of an hour, but was unable to locate the law firm. I was frustrated and annoyed and then decided to return home. Consequently, the divorce papers that I attempted to file were never processed. I will now share the significance of this experience.

At the time, I could not understand the strange unfolding of events. I was angry and frustrated. It was much later that a spiritual leader reminded me that if you file for divorce for reasons other than abuse or adultery, then you are not free to re-marry, as you may be perceived as living in perpetual adultery. This perspective might be controversial or unpopular in many circles. Anyway, seven years after my first marriage, my ex-husband filed for divorce on the grounds of irreconcilable differences. I was free to re-marry, and I did!

Ladies, take heed to wise counsel. Pay attention to the warning signs and trust your gut. If you must fight too hard for something, maybe it was never meant to be. You do not lose what you never had in the first place. Tell that to any naïve twenty-two-year-old!

The Hard Times

After my divorce, I found it hard to focus—I withdrew from college and attempted to sustain employment. I frequently found myself in the hospital because I was not taking care of myself. At the back of my mind I could still hear my wise old friend Daisy's voice reverberating in my ears as she quipped, "You never truly recover from a nervous breakdown."

I self-sabotaged my job opportunities—I landed great placements but suffered from the loss of my first marriage. I missed days from work and had my temporary contracts rescinded because I was invariably absent. Never one with a delicate constitution, I somehow seemed to get sick at the most inconvenient times.

My cardiologist was stumped—he could not figure out why I was an under-thirty-year-old, normal weight, non-smoker and nondrinker with heart problems. I wore a Halter monitor for two days to monitor my heart. I was then diagnosed with mitral valve prolapse. This diagnosis meant that I had to take antibiotics if I was going for routine dental appointments. I was put on lifetime beta blockers.

I found myself with the impossible decision of continuing my education or getting a full-time job to support myself. I struggled to stay in school—so I decided to take a semester off from school. That one semester morphed into years—the two-time valedictorian became a college drop-out!

Second Chances

During my sabbatical from school, other personal and professional doors mysteriously opened for me. I got my second chance at love. I met and married the love of my life. More about that later...

I encountered many roadblocks and challenges over the course of several years. After multiple and sustained layoffs, company mergers, and acquisitions, I was at a career crossroads. During the hard times, my older sister always stepped in to help us. I will always be grateful for her generosity, love, and unconditional kindness. God has been faithful. He always made a way out of no way. I have developed unconditional trust and unwavering faith in God. I know He always saw me in my difficult circumstances.

Hubris

I struggled with pride—I would suffer in silence instead of reaching out to my family for help. As I have reflected on the hard times, the bad financial decisions, and the residual obligations from my previous marriage, I have recalled times when I struggled financially. Throughout the years, the Lord has humbled me and shown me that humility is the highest form of leadership; vulnerability is indeed quiet strength.

Vulnerability

I have grown personally and professionally. I now realize the power of vulnerability, taking risks, making unpopular decisions, and exposing myself to hurt, ridicule, and judgment (Brown 2013). I am a strong proponent of vulnerability—I concur that vulnerability is really strength. I also subscribe to the theory of emotional intelligence (Goleman 1995) and the value of being self-aware. I am aware of what's happening around me and have learned to control my emotions and use them to my advantage to inspire positive change undergirded with respect and trust. Tony Robbins argues that "there are no negative emotions"; what matters is how we interpret the emotions.

Emotional Intelligence (EIQ)/ Positive Intelligence (Goleman 1995)

Over the years, I've learned to master my emotions—my siblings and I inherited our father's passion and slow-rising but ultimately explosive temper. Like my father, I would sometimes go from zero to a hundred in five seconds. This personality flaw is the explosive kind of anger with negative consequences—there were instances where I would not restrain what I was thinking and verbalizing. As a result of this bad temper, I recently walked away from a six- figure executive position, as I had gotten to the point where I could not suffer fools gladly anymore! I quit without having another job to go to. I needed to improve my positive intelligence and self-control!

Difficult Findings

People are uncomfortable with conversations about religion, race, class, and gender. I can attest to the difference between equity and equality in this culture. In the acclaimed movie *A Few Good Men* (Sorkin 1992), the lead actor barked, "You can't handle the truth!" He was right! Sometimes, I felt bullied in the boardroom. When I spoke up, I used to worry that I would be perceived as the "angry black woman" because invariably, I was the only black woman in the boardroom in various jobs, over many years. I recall that while being eight months pregnant with my daughter, I was bullied by an awful boss who told me that if I was late one more time he would "dock me," although I was a salaried employee at the time. I remember at my next Ob/Gyn visit I was so emotionally stressed that my doctor put me on bedrest for the remainder of my pregnancy.

Disappointing Encounters

When I was about fourteen years old, I went for a sleepover at one of my friend's houses. That night, I awakened to the stench of alcohol, and I observed her uncle coming into the room, slurring his words, and walking unevenly. I realized at this point that I was no match for this man, because he was huge—well over six feet and sturdily built. I was very petite and probably eighty-five pounds at that time. Somehow, I managed to navigate my way around him, and I ran to my girlfriend, who woke up. I told her what had happened, and she apologized profusely for her uncle's actions. I always told myself I'd never go back to sleep over with that friend, because I knew I could not predict the behavior of her family members.

Chapter 22

Back-up Plan

Conversely, while being pregnant with my son, I had an executive role where I was the corporate finance manager, leading fourteen branches. During a monthly presentation to the senior leadership team, somehow the PowerPoint slides failed to cooperate, and the technology did not work. Being heavily pregnant, with hyperactive hormones, I dissolved into tears. My CFO said to me gently, "Karen, what could we have done differently?" From then on, I learned to always have a back-up plan!

I have resolved to always think ahead, strategize, and plan in advance, because preparation meeting opportunity is the true essence of success, as I've learned over the years. I've also developed a strong sense of punctuality—"early is on time, on time is late, and late is unacceptable" has become my mission statement (L. Brown n.d.).

Pre-mature Data Analysis—Temporarily Stepping Out of God's Will

Satan has tried to hijack my future several times. I remember back in the early 2000s that within six months of arriving at a certain university, I quit my job. I felt disrespected and unappreciated for my worth to the team—my white counterparts would arrive at work at noon, while my boss had me driving almost an hour to be at work by 7:00 a.m. I remember the nurses in the research center would say to me, "Why are you here so early?" or "Can we have breakfast first?" To which I would say, lamely, "But my patients are scheduled for 7 o'clock."

After several months of doing this tough commute and receiving unfair and unequal treatment compared to my white counterparts, I turned in my resignation. To which my manager replied, "What can I do to make it better for you?" She flatly refused to take my resignation.

I thank God that she didn't accept my resignation, because I would have hijacked my future and I would have hijacked my daughter's scholarship, which paid seventy-five percent of her $250,000 tuition. This university also paid for my master's degree in epidemiology.

Chapter 23

Friends

"A lifetime's not too long/To live as friends" (Smith n.d.)

I remember meeting CD during my first year at a prestigious university. She was my "ride or die" who touched my life in a phenomenal way. I remember her telling me, "You should start your doctorate!" or "Even one course per semester." I later learned that this was her gift to all of her "mentees." She taught me so much! I will be forever grateful for her love and support at the start of my academic career. She changed my life forever. Unfortunately, CD struggled with health challenges and had a massive heart attack in her forties. I still remember her, with her big spirit and *weird* insecurities about her job. She was a prolific writer and researcher whose career ended prematurely.

We commiserated with each other when we felt suffocated by invisible saboteurs in academia. We surmised that certain key personnel were threatened by strong, black, well-educated women— we were bullied and passed over at every turn. CD always confided that despite our credentials, she felt that "we were not white enough." CD's fate reminds me that health care providers need to take better care of themselves, especially when they have preventable chronic illnesses. We need to love ourselves and take care of ourselves and practice what we preach. We must be accountable to each other for seeking and maintaining holistic health and wellness.

Limitations to Study Findings

Harsh Realities

Institutional racism is rampant, especially in academia, "a place where dreams go to die." It was not unusual for me to see people of color in positions of servitude, whether they were groundskeepers, security guards, ancillary staff, facility workers, or janitors. My daughter would often remark to me, "Mom, why are all the black people in the menial jobs?" She innocently exaggerated, as not all minorities were in low-paying jobs. Of course, there were some non-white employees in the upper echelons of academia—persons who broke through the mold and became accomplished doctors and faculty members. However, we still have a huge racial divide and observe disparities in the way the black people are relegated to positions of lower status. Even well-educated black people, like myself, must fight to advance, obtain social mobility, and acquire positions of influence, while our white counterparts are often handed things on a platter or wear the "backpack of white privilege."

Academic Disparities

I will never forget a black work-study student on my research team. He wanted to do medicine; however, he experienced overt discrimination, and he would share with me about the unfair and disparate treatment from the white faculty to the black students and how he always felt marginalized. Several semesters later, I saw him on campus. To my surprise, he informed me that he'd had to switch his major from pre-medicine to pre-nursing. I was so disappointed! I knew that he could make a difference, but he didn't fight hard enough. Nursing is a noble profession, but I know he could have done great things in the field of medicine.

When I immigrated from Jamaica to the United States, the expectation was that I would go to medical school. Nursing was a "Plan B." But it is the best decision I ever made. Like the popular advertisement, "I'm proud to be a nurse!"

Homogenous Associations

I have been blessed with many good friends. I have had one good girlfriend whom I regarded as my "ride or die," my radical and rebellious friend who sweetened my life for a season. My life was disrupted by the loss of a significant girlfriend whom I dearly loved. My other effervescent and charming girlfriend was the social butterfly who made sure we had scheduled girl's nights, trips, or sleepovers. Over the years, we all grew apart.

For example, my gourmet chef friend taught us how to do the electric slide and never missed an opportunity to celebrate. I will miss the relationships I cherished. My lifelong friends continue to be celebrated and continue to be there during the good and bad times. I continue to learn from the purposeful relationships; the shallow relationships will not be prolonged. Thank you, God, for the different types of friendships and relationships—I cherish all of them.

Disneyland Paris

I remember the year we took a girls' trip to Disneyland Paris. We literally just walked up to the rides—there were no lines like in Orlando. What a great time of bonding and being children all over again, with Disney character breakfasts and just having a good time.

Encounter with Camel on the Pyramids

Another time, my girlfriend and I traveled to Egypt. We danced and splashed in the Red Sea and dramatized Moses' and the Israelites' miraculous crossing. I remember us climbing on the camels. How frightened I was when I realized that the camels were only kneeling, and as soon as they rose to their full height, I was shocked at how tall they were! I sat precariously on the camel, and I was not a happy camper.

Once when we were traveling, we were bumped from a flight. My daughter, who was six years old at the time, could not understand why we were not seated in first class, as the plane was clearly empty. We spent the night sleeping in the airport in London. With the children being so adventurous, they had a great time, while the adults were not happy about the delay in getting back to the United States.

Part 5

Divine Encounters

Chapter 24

Divine Intervention

Satan tried to take my son on more than five occasions that come to mind. First, when I used to work from home, and my office was downstairs, I recall thinking, *It's way too quiet!* I could not see my eighteen-month-old child. I climbed the stairs two at a time—when I got to the master bathroom, I froze in my tracks! My toddler had managed to fill the Jacuzzi with water, and I'm amazed that he didn't drown, because he was so top-heavy—his eighteen-month-old head seemed very big for his body. Anyway, he had managed to remove all the new diapers from the storage container and had thrown all the new diapers into the jacuzzi filled with water. The bloated diapers looked like floating ducks. I was amazed at how much water the diapers could hold. Thank God that he was mesmerized by this illusion of floating ducks, as this distraction turned out to be a blessing that saved him from drowning. At first, I was a little sad because the whole pack of diapers I had just bought were ruined, but I thank God that he didn't topple in or try to get in. God had saved his life.

On another occasion, my sister and her family were visiting from out of town, and we took all the children for a planned outing to the lake. After missing several turns, we decided to return to the neighborhood swimming pool. Shane was about two years old. I told him and his cousin Justine to stay at the edge of the pool because they did not yet know how to swim. My sisters and I were chatting and having a great time catching up. I remember hearing my niece say, in an amazed way, "Look at Shane!"

When I glanced over to the swimming pool, I was just in time to see my son's head bobbing as he went under a couple of times. Without a moment's hesitation, I jumped into the pool, fully clothed, and grabbed him. Thank God, he wasn't scared and didn't panic. When I pulled him to the ground and attempted to perform CPR on him, he was fine, and he quickly recovered. Upon reflection, this had to be divine providence—the plan for us was to go to the huge, hundred-mile natural lake to which people gravitated in the summer. Even though we had gone there several times, I remember that on this day my sister and I kept getting lost, and we were so frustrated that finally we decided to return to the neighborhood pool. I shudder to think what could've happened that day had we made it to the lake, because the outcome could've been tragically different. If my son had wandered away into that lake, he could have drowned. I know that divine intervention saved his life that day!

Day at the Park and Another Brush with Death

On another occasion, I had taken my children, Shenelle and Shane, to the park as we normally do. My husband was outside walking the dog, because pets were not permitted near the swing sets. I was distracted for a moment and somehow looked up in time to see Shane walking in the path of the returning swing—he was behind the swings almost at the same time that Shenelle was charging backward in the swing. As Shane walked into the pathway of the advancing swing, Shenelle's body just crashed into him at a high rate of speed and knocked him over. Shane fell to the ground, his eyes rolled over, and the wind was knocked out of him.

I screamed for help, and my husband came running. He wanted to take my son in the car, and I had the presence of mind to call 911. When Shane got to the children's hospital, he revived, and thank God there was no permanent damage. Again, God had stepped in and saved him.

I recall when Shane was one day old, and I was nursing him. I happened to look down at my baby just in time to see his eyes rolling to the back of his head. I panicked and called 911. It turned out that the Percocet I had taken for pain control was expressed in the breastmilk, and my son was getting all the psychotropic medication while he nursed. Once again, God intervened to save his life.

School Bus Incident

On another occasion, I picked up Shenelle from the bus stop, and Shane, the happy toddler that he was, ran in front of the traffic and almost got run over by a car. I remember taking him home and spanking him because I was so scared that I had almost lost him, and I warned him to always listen to me and to be obedient. Again, his life was spared. Fast-forward to his freshman college years. During Shane's freshman year, he struggled with the new normal of college away from home. He confided to his sister that he had struggled with acclimating to college and was nearing a breaking point.

Concussions Interrupted

I thank God for intervening in his life once again, and today, he is a healthy, happy, well-adjusted and responsible twenty-one-year-old. To God be the glory. There are times when Shane played football, and because he was such a good running back, his rivals would try to grab his legs as they all targeted him. He would come home sometimes and tell me, "Oh, you know, I got hit in my head and I can't even remember when!" I was so worried about concussions that when he no longer played football, I said thank you, Jesus. One day, Shane was on his skateboard in the neighborhood and decided to pick the steepest hill to lunge. As he careened down the hill, he almost got hit by an oncoming car while he was skateboarding. Again, God saved his life!

Chapter 25
Resilience

Toughest Little Fragile Girl

My friend "Angel" was a prayer warrior and the toughest little fragile girl I knew. She loved to sing and dance. Her children were her pride and joy. She had survived a rough childhood and an abusive marriage. She developed a steadfast faith in Christ. Unfortunately, I moved to another state, and though we tried to reconnect at every available opportunity, our friendship died a slow and painful death.

She fought her demons at home and work, and invariably worked in environments where she was bullied and unappreciated. She loved to work out, and she was physically and mentally strong. She pushed herself beyond her limits. She was very conscientious about what she ate and just lived a positive life. She had survived a very difficult childhood, and the demons still tormented her in terms of her self-worth and what she could be.

I remember one instance where she was on the phone, and she confided that she was suicidal. She was in a very abusive marriage, and her husband was using drugs.

I counselled and begged and pleaded with my friend for several hours as I tried to "talk her off the ledge," literally and figuratively. After much intercession, I felt confident that she would not harm herself, and so I hung up the phone. I had no idea how emotionally and physically drained I was until I collapsed on the floor and had to call 911. I was admitted to the hospital for severe stress.

Hydrotherapy Friend

It seems for many years I found myself diagnosed with walking pneumonia. It dawned on me that I would take hot showers, not chase with cold showers, and thus not close my pores. I would then walk out into the cold air during the wintertime. No wonder I was sick with pneumonia. Several years after, a friend shared with me a technique called *hydrotherapy*, where you take several hot showers—as hot as you can stand—followed by cold, and alternating them. This is a practice that I've used for over twenty years. Knock on wood, no more pneumonia.

Chapter 26

Miracle at the Gas Station

Lunch, or Gas?

At one point in my life, I found myself floundering. Nothing seemed to work. I hit a rough patch where I found myself in-between jobs. I eventually obtained a temporary contract. I remember driving out to work one day, and I only had five dollars in my pocket. I debated whether I should buy lunch or put gas in my tank, which normally cost $18 to fill, with only five dollars to my name. Common sense prevailed, so I knew that I had to get the gas in order to get back home. I drove to the gas station and proceeded to pre-pay for $5 of gas.

Forget About the Pennies

Since I only had five dollars, I pre-paid the attendant and proceeded to pump the gas. To my amazement, the pump kept going, and going, and going, until the tank overflowed and spilled onto my boots, splashing the hem of my winter coat. I was mad! This was in the dead of winter. I remember being a little annoyed because I had pre-paid the gas, and I wondered where I would get the money to pay the difference.

I walked back to the office and snapped at the attendant. I told him that the tank was full! He said, "No, look on the computer." I was amazed. According to his computer, the pump was showing only $5.03 due—he said, "Forget about the pennies!"

As I walked back to my car, I expected them to call me at any moment to say there was some mistake, but it never happened. So, I quickly drove away and returned to the office, where I shared story with my boss. He replied confidently, "It's definitely the Man upstairs!" That was my first tangible miracle among many.

Chapter 27

My Philosophy

We should be optimists and see the glass as half-full—never empty.
Think about authentic happiness or positive psychology—remember, we are arbiters of our own happiness. We are not dependent on others; we should seek out opportunities to constantly refill our glasses. We have all the resources we need to figuratively fill our glasses! So, we should operate from a sphere of overflow and abundance. If we can think it, we can see it; if we can see it, we can believe it! Also, the Bible reminds us that God wants to give us abundant life.[xl]

Moreover, just think of the value of cultivating a spirit of gratitude and abundance; think of the abundant things that we enjoy that others less fortunate don't possess. We live in the richest and most blessed population in earth's history; think of the resources that are at our disposal: technology; sophisticated procedures and advances in medicine to combat chronic diseases; advances in treatment and medical technology. With this litany of resources that we have access to, we should celebrate!

See the World through Rose-Colored Lenses

It is important to note that resilience, joy, appreciation, and making a conscious effort and choice to be happy often yields high dividends. It is well established that implementing good sleep hygiene also makes you feel better. A single positive change that we can make in our lives is to minimize negative emotions and to control how we choose to respond to negative situations. We should take a few moments each day to express what we are grateful for.

By adopting a positive outlook, smiling, and positively engaging, we will change our brain chemistry. We have much so power over our circumstances—and most of all, we have all the ingredients for happiness and success if we reach deep inside and surrender to the

One who is in control of our lives.

Gratitude Journaling

We are encouraged to practice saying three new things for which we are grateful, for twenty-one days, to increase our optimism and enrich our environment. Gratitude changes the vibrational frequency in the world and what we draw to ourselves (Beckwith n.d.). Research suggests that recalling one meaningful thing that's happened to you over the last twenty-four hours or focusing on something meaningful for two minutes will get your brain to relive the experience as it leads to visualization versus accelerated actualization (Achor n.d.). That brings me to one of the things that I am most grateful for in my life— my immediate and extended family!

Part 6

Family Connections

Chapter 28

My Immediate Family

Winston

Winston and I share a special bond—we are truly soulmates. Winston treats me like a queen: breakfast in bed, walks on the beach, walks on the nature trail, watching a movie, just curling up on the couch in front of the fireplace on winter evenings, going to church, serving others, reading together, and praying together. With an unconditional love, it's been twenty-seven years. We only dated for three months—people thought this marriage would not stand a chance or that we were crazy, but we've been blessed. We subscribe to a higher faith, knowing that nothing is impossible when you put your trust in God.

Our special song:

Sometimes when I look back to yesterday
When I lost my way home
Caught up in rivers of dreams
Oceans of promises
That leave you alone
And though we don't understand
But we know that it's true
How our God will use circumstances to speak to you!
You turned my stumbling block to a stepping-stone
You loved me even though You knew I was wrong
Oh Lord you never cease to amaze me!

Your loving arms became a bridge of mercy
You turned my stumbling block to a stepping-stone.

Life is a garden of trials and failures
Sometimes you slip up and fall
But in the midst of a storm
When you needed someone
That's when my Jesus stands tall.
I know that God won't leave you
In a time of despair
You're like a flower that's broken
And you need special care.
Just let Him...

He'll turn your stumbling block to a stepping-stone
He'll love you even though He knew you were wrong
Oh, Lord you never cease to amaze me!
Your loving arms became a bridge of mercy
You turned my stumbling block to a stepping-stone!

I know God has angels
Who are holding my hands
Cause the Lord surely knows
I want to stand like a (wo)man
But whenever I stumble
I'm going reach up to you.
There is only one thing to do
Just let Him turn your stumbling block into a stepping-stone!
~ Words by (Giants n.d.)

Daughter of Mine

Shenelle is so funny! When she was about eighteen months old, I remember I went to the hairdresser to get my hair styled. After neglecting myself, as new mothers are prone to do, I had the nerve to upgrade to a *beehive* hairdo, which was quite popular back then. She had fallen asleep at the salon and slept soundly when I put her back in her car seat. As we were driving on the highway, I glanced back at her, at which point she woke up and freaked out, as if she somehow failed to recognize me—I guess I was transformed by the new hairdo!

When she looked at me, she just cried and cried. She seemed frightened and could not be consoled. I had to pull over to the side of the highway, and I tried to reassure her that I was still her mother. When that didn't work, I decided to remove the hairpins that secured my beehive, and I said coaxingly, "See, it's me, Mommy!" She finally recognized me when I had restyled my hair into the boring ponytail.

About three months later, my niece was babysitting Shenelle. When I picked her up, she started to throw up uncontrollably. We took her to the hospital, where they did many tests, and they could not figure out what was wrong with her. The fever refused to abate, and the vomiting could not be controlled. In desperation, the doctors restrained her as they attempted to do a spinal tap. My poor niece was apologetic and said she had watched her carefully. She insisted that Shenelle had not ingested anything poisonous. To this day, we still don't know what happened to her, but thank God she recovered and is such an accomplished young lady today.

Shenelle is brilliant—she started to read fluently before she turned three years old. She would pick up CDs and read the lyrics as she sang along with Michael Bolton, Babyface, Mariah Carey, and Bebe and Cece Winans. In church, she had the strongest, loudest voice. I remember the pastor thanking her one Sabbath for her strong contribution to the song service. She was undoubtedly the most confident reader among her peers, and invariably the teachers selected her to read the children's story for church.

She was in the talented and gifted program. She was a strong performer, and she was selected as a finalist for the National Merit Scholarship because her PSAT scores were so strong. At the graduation ceremony, she was easily the student with the most scholarships. Someone remarked that she had gotten all the scholarships! We decided on a prestigious local university because I wanted her close to home. She graduated in the top one hundred seniors and continues to do very well.

From the age of two years, Shenelle began traveling to Jamaica every summer to stay with her aunt. It was a welcome respite for me, the perpetual student. I could focus on my studies because I was the perpetual student and the summer breaks were a blessing. It allowed me a chance to reconnect with my soulmate, because Shenelle came right after we got married.

My Son

Shane pulls at my heartstrings effortlessly. I love my Shane. He is fierce, tough, and a deep thinker. He will say the most thoughtful thing at the most opportune time. He is wise beyond his years. At two, his prayers would leave you breathless. We knew he was going to be a pastor or a minister, or choose a career path to inspire millions. He could see God in nature, while flying on an airplane, or in the most mundane things.

When Shane was a toddler on vacation in Jamaica, my aunt hired a nanny for him. After frustration with multiple diaper changes, the nanny must have gently scolded him. My sister tells me that they were shocked when the barely two-year-old retorted, "Everyone has to poop!"

In contrast to Shenelle's eighteen hours of labor, Shane was ready for the world. He was born within three hours of labor—that includes the time when my water broke, travel to the hospital, and getting checked into the labor and delivery suite. Shane was ready to make his appearance—I remember that his dad and sister went to get McDonald's for breakfast on the first floor of the hospital. By the time they returned to the room, Shane was born. That's my boy, ready to face the world—a beautiful little sumo wrestler who was so big, he could not fit into his size "newborn" baby clothes.

My four-legged child is Lila. Lila, our golden retriever mix, has been such a joy to us. Over the years, we have had some goldfish, a beta fish, two lovebirds, a chocolate Lab, a terrier mix, and my impish cats, Alex and Nicky. I have had my share of fur babies.

Chapter 29

Correlations

Little did I realize it then, but I am blessed to be part of a rich pedigree consisting of six phenomenal sisters, five of whom are "C-Suite" executives, and my outstanding brothers, four of whom are entrepreneurs much like our father.

My journey was punctuated by the love and kindness of family. For example, my second oldest sister is generous, thoughtful, and loving. I recall driving home from school one day, not knowing where the money would come from to pay for my tuition or for my books. The phone rang serendipitously—it was my older sister. I confided in her, and she told me not to worry about it. The next day, she deposited thousands of dollars in my bank account.

During another dark chapter in my life, she called. The consummate prayer warrior, she prophesied to me that God had already restored me and screamed like a woman in travail that restoration was coming my way.

Similarly, another prayer warrior sister is blessed with the power of discernment, and she can see the truth a mile away. She could be thousands of miles away, but she could tell you exactly what was going in your life. She is blessed with self-awareness and discernment to influence others. I thank God for using these phenomenal women to bless my life!

Divine Providence or Appointment with a Destiny Chaser

By a series of circumstances, I was searching for inspirational videos, and as I was flipping channels I came across a motivational speaker. The topic of her presentation was attention grabbing—it was something along the lines of how to be a better public speaker. I am always seeking opportunities to hone my craft and better develop myself. I had never heard of her, but I was mesmerized by her transparency, humility, and vulnerability as I watched video after video. Pretty soon, I was conversant with her incredible "rags to riches" story. I started to share with my siblings how she had inspired me. I knew I had to write my story. I felt impressed to purchase her books, and so I proceeded to order them online.

I intended to use my daughter's Amazon Prime account, and so I asked her to order the books for me. I mentioned a certain book to which she replied, "Mom, I have that book—I just finished reading it! I told you I wanted you to read it, remember?" I vaguely recalled the conversation. Anyway, my son picked up the book from his sister and delivered it to me. Not surprisingly, the book was autographed by my sister. More amazing to me, I opened the book and saw that it was signed 2009, approximately ten years prior.

I was amazed that I'd never heard of this book in over a decade! Moreover, I was disappointed that my sister had not shared the book with me. According to worldly standards, my sister is accomplished. She has lived and continues to live an abundant life!

I cannot wait to share this book with those within my sphere of influence—I feel like if I had I read the book or watched the movie I would have hosted screening parties and book club soirees. I immediately discussed with my immediate family the wealth of knowledge and good experiences found with in the book. In fact, within a day of watching the film and reading the book, I got a job offer for a part-time position which has morphed into full time.

Divine Appointments

It was motivation and inspiration that encouraged me to start writing my book. As this author would say, "No one else can write your story." I owe her a debt of gratitude for inspiring me to take on this task. I know that the spirit of abundance is around me. I know that positivity surrounds me as I subscribe to the *positivity* and *abundance*. I am more attuned to my thoughts, now knowing that the thoughts morph into actions.

By reading and watching these inspirational pieces, I feel more self-actualized into a better woman, more vulnerable, more in touch with my myself. I have become more spiritually aware and now immerse myself in the spirit of gratitude and abundance. I claim all the wealth and goodness that the universe has to offer me. Moreover, the Bible[xli] tells us "I am come that you might have life and have it more abundantly!"

Part 7

Career Changes and Transitions

Chapter 30

Career Crossroads

From Nursing Assistant to Chief Nursing Administrator

When I arrived in Atlanta I was desperate to seek a job, and I contracted with a healthcare job placement agency. My first assignment was to go to a nursing home, for which I would receive *per diem* compensation. I remember driving through an affluent neighborhood with manicured lawns and mansions boasting of European architecture before arriving at my destination.

A day in the life of a nursing assistant consisted of diaper changes, feeding, and walking older adults, and the occasional assault by a combative or confused resident. At the end of this first day, I decided that this was not the occupation for me. It was then that I decided to embark on a nursing career. I worked for an assisted living facility as a medical technician, where I dispensed medications to the residents on evenings and weekends. I also assisted with the activities of daily living.

During my last semester of nursing school, I became a nurse extern, or patient care technician (PCT), and upon graduation and successfully passing the National Licensure Examination or "boards," I received my professional nursing license. After two years at the bedside I realized that I wanted to broaden my nursing skills, and so I embarked on a doctoral program, and later completed a PhD in nursing.

Career Crossroads

After thirteen years in strategic management and finance, punctuated by working with companies that were acquired or which relocated out of state, I decided to change my career trajectory. At the prodding of my older siblings, I returned to school to pursue a career in nursing. Prior to completing my nursing career, I briefly switched careers and tried to complete a degree in computer science. I soon discovered that computer programming was not for me and gravitated to psychology, at which I excelled. I majored in psychology and minored in gerontology.

I was later introduced to a new program in gerontology which took me to Georgia State University, and my thesis chair later recommended that I transition into clinical research. This decision turned out to be fortuitous—I was at a prestigious research university for twelve years, and then I worked for a national university, where I became the chief nursing administrator.

Chapter 31

More Protocol Deviations

Times of Loss Punctuated My Life

At twelve years old, I lost my best friend in high school, Sharon. She was the sweetest, gentlest friend. Sharon suffered from a congenital heart condition, and she could not participate in physical education or typical school activities. Also, the steroids that she took caused her body to swell. She was in and out of school for the first year, and by the time summer break began, she had passed. I had gone away to another parish.

When I returned to school, I was told that she had passed away. I was heartbroken because I didn't get a chance to say goodbye or to have closure. To add insult to injury, my aunt passed away from cancer. My aunt had shared the hospital room with Sharon. I remember I would visit them on the weekend—that was a tough time!

I lost my grandmother after graduating from high school. Fast-forward twenty years: I lost my mother-in-law, two brothers-in-law, and then seven years later my best friend from cancer.

Compromised Data

My best friend "Cherubim" walked into my life unexpectedly. She was a brave, phenomenal woman who left her homeland to seek opportunities for her family. After pursuing a career opportunity which did not pan out, she decided to remain in the United States to explore other opportunities. At some point in time, she had obtained another job and saved up funds, so she was able to send money for her family.

Victimized by the Health Care Delivery System

Cherubim's family joined her in the United States, but once again the job opportunity was not what she expected. She grieved her previous lifestyle and the family she had left behind. She regretted her ill-fated decision to immigrate to the United States. She used to live in a beautiful home there; she had to settle for low-paying jobs here, for which she was overqualified. She would trade office work at a school so her children could have their tuition waived. After a series of unfortunate circumstances, she was diagnosed with breast cancer. She fought a valiant fight but eventually succumbed to her illness.

One hospital wreaked havoc on her body—she had a botched mastectomy. One year after the procedure, as I assisted to change her dressings, I literally saw staples falling from her mangled breast. How she suffered! Her hemoglobin levels were always precariously low, and she would frequently be out of breath to the point of passing out. She had multiple transfusions and would be discharged in the dead of night. I slept over at her house many nights and kept her company. She was too tired to wage a legal fight.

It was such a devastating time, because she always held onto the belief that she would be healed, but unfortunately this was not a part of the plan. My friend's fight with cancer had me questioning everything I knew, because she was a vegetarian, she ran five miles a day, she used a non-traditional anti-perspirant, and most of all, she was a woman of faith. She loved playing the piano; she was a connoisseur of music. People left her bedside feeling inspired because of the incredible faith that she had that she would be healed. I will never forget my friend!

I lost both parents and my father-in-law within the space of a year and a half. These losses took a toll on my family emotionally, financially, and psychologically. I've learned that life is not promised, and we should celebrate every milestone and love passionately and deeply, because we never know when loved ones may be taken prematurely.

Part 8

Study Discussion

Chapter 32

Non-Negotiable Faith

"I'm so sorry, you didn't make it!" The harsh words reverberated in my ears. Incredulously, I asked, "What did you say?" The professor repeated, "I am so sorry, you didn't make it." It was a bitter pill to swallow. I had worked so hard for my senior check-off, only to be told that it wasn't good enough. What was even more frustrating was the fact that the points which were deducted from my overall score related to the fact that *my stethoscope was dangling.*

This final decision effectively blocked my graduation—this decision was even more frustrating because we were using plastic simulation *manikins*—not to be confused with mannequins—and it was not unusual for stethoscopes not to have a snug fit. It was devastating news to be told that I had failed the clinical check-off because of that quirk. I appealed the decision, but my protests were rejected, and I soon realized that it was pointless to argue with the professor.

I spent the whole weekend in the fetal position, because I realized I would need to wait another semester in order to graduate. I was inconsolable. I remember my best friend, who was terminally ill at the time, was planning to attend my graduation in a wheelchair. When I explained to her that I needed to wait another semester, she consoled me and encouraged me to "not kick against the pricks." She was so understanding and comforting. Nevertheless, this was a tough lesson to learn. Fear of failure is not an option, even for circumstances beyond one's control!

I was so disappointed and bitter that I did not even take my graduation pictures! I refused to walk across the stage. I refused to participate in other events that the seniors were participating in. After finally graduating from nursing school, I worked at bedside for a couple of years and then I resolved to go back to graduate school. This decision propelled me into another career with a prestigious university in the Southeast.

Study Validation

Fast-forward to April 2010, when my dissertation defense announcement was disseminated. Certain key personnel balked at the fact that I had completed my doctoral requirements within two and a half years. Despite my fully executed data use agreement, a senior adviser demanded that we review my data with a fine-tooth comb. Despite my pristine data, my reviewer informed me that crucial regulatory documents were not in order. In fact, she told me that my dissertation would be invalidated because she could not find an authorization from the Institutional Review Board (IRB) authorizing me to conduct my research.

The forced delay in my dissertation defense was inconvenient, given that all my files were in order. I was meticulous in my research management and observed all research protocols. Notwithstanding, upon reviewing my list of approvals, somehow my most critical dissertation approval was missing from the binder. I immediately identified this as *spiritual warfare* and prayed about it. It appeared that legions of demons were released into my dissertation committee deliberations.

After a three-month delay with my dissertation defense, the committee did not see any irregularities and acknowledged that I did not deviate from regulatory guidelines. Hence, my dissertation was re-instated. I was able to conduct the final defense of my dissertation in August 2010. This achievement was bittersweet, because most of my family had arrived in Atlanta for a major convention—this was supposed to be a dual celebration, with family arriving from outside the United States. The delay resulted in my family missing the PhD graduation celebration with me.

I should not have been surprised, because with each of my previous degrees, I always encountered roadblocks at the time of graduation. This happened with my nursing degree, my psychology degree, my first master's degree, and my second master's degree. In fact, a committee chair covertly distorted my manuscript. I am thankful that I had witnesses to this evil behavior. By some supernatural force, I made the deadline to submit my manuscript in the nick of time! Nevertheless, I persevered and overcame the obstacles to reap my true rewards.

No Weapons Formed Against You Will Prosper

Prayer has always been my constant—part of my trifecta of praise, prayer, and psalms. When I was confused or excited or hurt or progressing, I always inserted prayer into my daily routine. I reached out to a member of the IRB team and graciously volunteered to go to the archives to retrieve my approval. Within twenty-four hours I had recovered a necessary approval that was missing, and my dissertation defense was scheduled. In something of a record timeframe, I was blessed to complete my PhD within two and a half years. I later accepted a post-doc fellowship in a coveted specialty. The post-doc fellowship came at a price, because I had to decline a job offer from a very powerful program chair, and she never let me forget it. In the years following that declined offer, I was blacklisted—she would never consider me for any positions for which I was qualified.

Chapter 33

Touch Not the Lord's Anointed

I experienced my share of discrimination and abuse in corporate America. In fact, I had no other choice but to hold one company accountable for the blatant racism and unfair treatment which was very pervasive in that culture then and now. I reported one company to the EEOC, and the reprisals persisted—my leadership then told me that we needed to part ways. They eventually settled the case with me.

Vindication does not take forever anymore—I am scared when I see people operate as if they are above the law, because the Bible talks about being fearfully and wonderfully made, and about not touching His anointed and doing His people no harm.[xlii]

Gratitude Journal

I thank God for days of prayer, fasting, and meditation. I have been blessed to have a closer walk with God. In one difficult situation after another, I saw God move in a miraculous way to fix my problem. There were also small tokens of blessings where it seemed like God was winking at me and reminding me that He has my back.

Fear of Failure

We should not fear failure—it allows us to take a new path, to go in another direction. I was blessed to hear a world-renowned neurosurgeon speak at my church—he shared his story about how he had struggled at Yale in undergraduate chemistry courses. Nothing clicked. He prayed, and one day the lights went on! He was able to succeed and was the first to separate conjoined twins in a miraculous surgery—the rest is history!

I also had the pleasure of listening to a prominent leader who shared his story of failure. He now boasts two doctoral degrees. He shared the story of how his PhD took him twenty years to complete. He shared how he had failed courses and was one step away from being dismissed from his program. He finally sat next to one of his classmates, and she tutored him. He was finally able to complete his dissertation, so do not fear failure. It can be a good thing, and in much the same way, change is the only constant—change is not a bad thing. Change causes growth—think of the metamorphosis of the caterpillar to the butterfly!

Biostatistics Nightmare

My daughter and I completed our master of public health degrees together. On one occasion, I was in a room with over one hundred students at Emory University. I was humbled to be surrounded brilliant students; some were half my age and were peers of my daughter who had matriculated there after their undergraduate degrees. I was mortified to discover that some of her friends were in my class. Fast-forward to the first biostatistics exam—somehow, I could not get my statistical program to run. The exam was slated to last an hour, and twenty minutes into the exam, I was frozen—my program refused to run. After the first forty minutes, I still had not started the first question. I was stuck!

My stomach started cramping and my bladder competed for my attention! My stomach growled like percussion instruments, and I was sweating profusely! I knew that if I failed that course I would have to wait another year to retake it, since it was only offered once per year. I was angry, frustrated, and nauseous.

Finally, I summoned enough courage to address the proctor, despite strict instructions not to ask for help or speak to the proctor, in order to protect the integrity of the exams. He had repeatedly told us not to communicate with him. Finally, I could take it no longer. I told him my statistical program was not working after trying for over forty minutes. He looked at the first line of my code and asked me what name I was using for the program. I said, "BMI, as in Body Mass Index," and he replied, "No, it is BM 1 (the number 1), not BMI—it's BM 1!"

My proctor discovered that someone had titled the SAS program BM1 (number 1) not BMI (letter I) which I kept reading as BMI (body mass index). By simply transposing that last character, I was messing up my program! So, finally, I was able to run my program, and I was able to pass my course. I can tell you that I sat in that room and I was sweating bullets. My body felt like Jell-O, and I told myself I could not afford to pass out because my daughter's friends were in the room with me. I would never be able to look them in the face again or overcome the humiliation of fainting (syncope) in my exam. Thank God I was able to move forward. Subsequently, my daughter and I crossed the stage together with our master's in public health degrees. We were interviewed by the school magazine and received a full article entitled "Like Mother, Like Daughter." That was one of the proudest moments in my life. To God be the glory!

Angel in the Classroom

When I returned to school for the final time to complete my MPH in epidemiology at Emory, it was a tough program. Sometimes I kicked myself and berated myself for being a glutton for punishment. It was a grueling and rigorous program. In one course, all semester long I sat in the same seat—I was invariably late for class, so I sat next to the exit of the auditorium. There were over 150 students in this competitive program. I worked full time, and with my many obligations, I often did not have time to attend the study sessions or office hours for the program.

As I sat for the final exam of the semester, I went into the room prepared to take my usual seat. I was disgusted to find someone sitting in *my seat!* A gentleman whom I had never seen all semester long was sitting in the seat. I grudgingly asked him why I had not seen him in the class before, and he nonchalantly responded that *he did not come to class.* Some students were practicing MDs, so I did not think this strange. What was strange were his next words—he unassumingly stated that I needed to make sure that I focused on certain questions, because they would be on the exam. I thought it strange, but felt it wouldn't hurt to review the material he recommended. I thanked him for the advice.

I proceeded to take my exam a few minutes later. To my amazement, every single question he recommended was on the exam, which I aced. He walked away, and I have never seen him since. I never saw him in any of my other courses for the remainder of the program. To this day, I think he was my angel in the classroom, sent to assist with my exam!

Chapter 34

Conclusion of the Matter

Respect authority, but don't be afraid to challenge the status quo. Be assertive, not arrogant; be brave, yet vulnerable! I had the effrontery to fire my first thesis chair because he was wasting my time and disrespecting me. I had already completed the graduate certificate in gerontology from one university and transferred those credits to the master's program. Due to external obligations, my thesis chair traveled almost all the time. The plan was for us to meet every two weeks. However, every time he met with me, he seemed to forget what we had discussed at the previous meeting. This went on for about six months.

Finally, I was so frustrated that one day that I think I scared him. I just told him, "I am done! I don't want to do this anymore," at which point he became unprofessional—he told me that my thesis had no merit and that my work was inferior. I refused to buy in to the false narrative. He was not going to define me or my work!

At that point, I reviewed the faculty directory and randomly selected a faculty—I just picked a name out of a hat. I reached out to her, and six months later my thesis was done! Later that year when I attempted to get my thesis bound, I encountered a weird series of events. My thesis formatting was warped, and the characters were eerily skewed. You cannot make this stuff up. I thought I was seeing things. Thankfully my sister, Jean, happened to be visiting me at the time. She confirmed what I suspected—my work was intentionally sabotaged—the document was corrupted. Thank God I had a copy preserved elsewhere.

Bad Recommendation Thwarted

Similarly, I had reached out to some faculty for recommendations for graduate school and got the first three, but somehow, there was a delay and overlap. I ended up having four instead of three. God was so good, because one faculty inadvertently gave me the recommendation unsealed, and I inadvertently opened it. To my amazement, it was negative and uncomplimentary. The professor stated that I was a good student but a terrible writer! I just discarded that recommendation letter, since I had already obtained adequate positive recommendations from the other faculty members. By divine providence, that negative recommendation letter came to me and never went to the graduate program admissions committee.

Fast-forward fifteen years—I literally wrote seven abstracts which were all accepted for presentation at national and international conferences. I was able to complete my doctorate in two and a half years and two master's degrees in record time (a six-year plan vs the traditional ten-year plan). Sometimes faculty members may attempt to hijack our future, intentionally or unintentionally, so we must be careful who we share our dreams with.

Chapter 35

Classic Study

Deep Trench Snailfish

I am fearfully and wonderfully made! [xliii] I believe it, because my Creator is a master designer. Think of the deep trench snailfish—according to National Geographic, this deep-sea creature can withstand more water pressure than 1,600 elephants standing on its head (Jameson 2017). Chinese researchers examined the anatomy and genetics of the fish and provided evidence that the fish has peculiarities to make them withstand intense pressure. For example, the fish have gaps in their skulls which help the internal and external pressures to be balanced. This balance is important, because as the fish does not have a complete and fused skull, so it cannot be crushed by the pressure.

I think God looked at my future and equipped me for the intense pressure and extreme temperatures I would face in my life. Like the deep trench snailfish, He has equipped me to withstand tumult and tragedy and to emerge unscathed. In the difficult times when God carried me, as in the famous *Footprints* poem, I emerged victorious and thankful for the lessons learned. It may sound cliché, but God doesn't give us more than we can bear, and with every temptation He makes a way of escape. Hallelujah!

Epilogue

Redemption and Restoration

Before I even knew about positive intelligence, I always knew that I had a friend in Jesus, and that I could take everything to Him in prayer. My mother gave me the example of prayer and fasting, so my life has been punctuated by worship and prayer. I never dared to deviate from this climate of worship, for fear that something bad would happen to me.

God has the final say! No matter what unjust and unfair circumstances we may encounter, I know that no one or nothing can put out our light without God's permission. I am humbled and honored when I think of the purpose for my life, and how I would have done myself a disservice by not sharing my story with others.

I am thrilled to articulate in vulnerability and strength the story of my personal triumph. I want to inspire others to go forward, claim their purpose, and chase their destiny, knowing that nothing is impossible. Knowing that God can take our little insignificant, ordinary lives and make them brilliant and extraordinary masterpieces. To God be the glory! Nothing happens by chance; everything is a part of God's master plan. I give God thanks as I look back and see how He was orchestrating all things *for my good*; He determined my destiny and purpose before I was even born, taking my feeble mortal clay and making my life beautiful and purposeful. As Maya Angelou exquisitely writes:

The Phenomenal Woman

Pretty women wonder where my secret lies.
I'm not cute or built to suit a fashion model's size
But when I start to tell them,
They think I'm telling lies.
I'm a woman

Phenomenally.
Phenomenal woman,
That's me.
Phenomenal woman,
That's me.

Now you understand
Just why my head's not bowed.

Afterword

Replicable Findings

I analyzed my life course data by adjusting for the confounding variables that were threats to my study validity. Undoubtedly the study findings were not due to chance, but showed the strength of pristine data meticulously collected over the years in this longitudinal study.

Observations confirmed my suspicions. My research questions were answered in the affirmative. Yes, the alternative hypothesis is true: that when you put your trust in God, all the resources of heaven are at your disposal. The God of the universe will move heaven and earth to perform His wonders in your life. My life study shows the beauty of non-negotiable faith. I borrowed spiritual theories in the translation of my research study to practice. The truth is the pragmatic. I am learning to create awareness that nothing is impossible with God, and that all things work together for good. The weapons formed, but did not prosper. I found unexpected results in the most expected places.

I have truly been an outlier, but I did not resist the study mean. The standards in my life showed that God will do exceedingly more than we can ask or think. I wrote my life story using the analogy of scientific theory to create awareness to explain and predict the relationship between ordinary people and extraordinary results. I have discovered that if you work in synergy with divine principles, and when your life aligns with the master designer, all things will work for your good.

I would be arrogant and presumptuous to believe that my study cannot be replicated, because I am by no means unique and what God has done for me, He can certainly do for others.

I serve a God who adds by subtracting and multiplies by dividing and defies logic. I have found that greater is He that is in me than he that is in the world. My God is omnipotent, omniscient, and

147

omnipresent, and when all the divine forces undergird my life, I can do exceedingly abundantly above all that I could ever ask or think.

Conclusion

Positive Results

Despite the study limitations of small sample size and limited generalizability, my life study findings may provide a deeper understanding of the relationship between ordinary people and extraordinary accomplishments. My study is important. All things do work together for our good.

In every situation and every aspect of my life, whether good or bad, I know that Jesus loves and cares for me. I know that I am never alone; I pull my strength from the assurance that Jesus sees everything that is happening to me. Moreover, without faith it is impossible to please God![xliv] I know that Jesus has me in the palm of His hands, and that He always had a plan for me no matter how resistant I was to His will.

I know, like the prodigal daughter, that God loves me and would always welcome me back with arms open wide. I know that, as Gloria Gaither wrote in her popular song: "I then shall live as one who's been forgiven... I am His child and I am not afraid!" That, like with little children, the song reverberates with me: "Yes, Jesus loves me/ Oh how He loves you and me/Yes, Jesus loves me."

I stand in amazement of all God has done for me. I claim His promises and continue to walk with boldness and authority, knowing that Jesus has my back. I have non-negotiable faith. When I give God something, I trust He will follow through. I cast all my cares at His feet; I submit all my plans to His will for my life. He reminds me also to pray for the unlovable, for those who do me wrong, and thus I operate in a sphere of peace—the peace that passes all understanding. My newfound peace defies logic; it is unfathomable that God loves me so much. All that I am, and all that I ever will be, is because of Him. This is my prayer, in the matchless name of Jesus. Amen.

Without change, no growth occurs. Consider the deep trench snailfish—although high pressures can also break down proteins, which are important for normal physiological processes, researchers found that the snailfish have high levels of a substance called trimethylamine N-oxide (TMAO), which is used to stabilize proteins (Jameson 2017). Most animals have one copy of these gene, while these fish have five. No matter—they can withstand intense external pressures! Like the snailfish, uniquely created with enough pressure inside to resist any external pressure, I have climbed the rough side of the mountain and emerged victorious. I chased my destiny and found redemption and restoration.

I remember I made a bold choice to leave a premier employer, which opened the pathway to another opportunity, which paved the way for supernatural favor in my current career trajectory. The Bible says I can do all things through Christ.[xlv] I am glad that I was bold and courageous enough to step out in faith even when the path was unclear, and even when I was unsure if I would have a pathway to success. The step of faith translated to triumph and victory.

I am walking in God's will, and I have found my purpose. I will continue to chase my destiny of ultimate success. I am reclaiming my purpose and enhancing my spirit. I have found the secret to wellness, prosperity, and abundance. I celebrate every milestone. Each day brings new blessings. I am growing in Jesus, for He is pointing me to the path. He is pointing me to the true north.

I live in gratitude; I welcome the open door to endless possibilities. I'm excited about my future. My non-negotiable, deliberate, daring faith has led me to the path to a joy-centered life—where all that's good and perfect is fulfilled in my purpose: the purpose of making a difference, touching lives, advocating for the disenfranchised, and inspiring others, one person at a time!

As I reflect on my life course, and the trajectory of my career, I am grateful for the object lessons, the difficult times, the brick walls, and the invisible glass ceilings. I know that God makes *all* things beautiful in His time. To God be the glory for the things He has done! Against the background of my secret weapon, my trifecta of praise, prayer, and psalms—if I had to do it all over again, my unwavering faith in God would always remain my only option, and undoubtedly, my non-negotiable!

Generativity

Future Directions

I can do all things through Christ! xlvi Whatever we can conceive and believe, we will achieve! So, I invite you to boldly step forward and claim all that God has in store for you. Identify the non-negotiable! Confidently embark on the faith-filled journey by aligning yourself with the omnipotent, omniscient source of all good things, the Almighty God!

God wants us to be completely dependent upon Him, because all that we are and everything that we've accomplished we could only have done through Christ. We should only be confident in God and the blessings and abilities that He has bestowed on us. Paul tells us that he counts all things as loss except for the excellence of the knowledge of Jesus Christ, and we should forget the things that are behind us and press toward the mark of the high calling of God in Christ! We must trust God that all things will work for our good!

Postscript

Life Study Implications

I would say: put God first in everything. Find what makes you happy and fulfilled—discover God's purpose for your life. Aspire to be a change agent—foster positive relationships, make time for community service, and be obedient to God's words. Be kind, loving, beautiful, receptive, and abundant. Forgive others and don't rush to judgment, because we do not always have all the facts. As in my life study, only the objective data is relevant. Stick to the facts. Love unconditionally, and be your best. Do not settle! Aspire to climb the second mountain, and you will come out victorious.

Epidemiologists study determinants of health and test for significant relationships to answer troubling questions, elucidate, illuminate, and explain elusive and spurious relationships among diseases and conditions that affect us globally. Quantitative researchers aim to accurately reject the null hypothesis in their conclusions about significant relationships. To avoid certain types of errors, researchers must be careful *not to reject a null hypothesis that is true* (Frankfort 2008). Thus, researchers may conduct bias analyses, to control for confounders or extraneous variables, and report scientific findings with much certainty. After conducting a bias analysis to address potential threats to validity of my life study, I am proud to report that, conditional on the accuracy of my bias-adjusted model, this destiny chaser, with God's authority, found a significant relationship in arriving at a place of victory.

Similarly, we must be willing to be humble, strong, vulnerable, patient, and transparent for God to fulfill His purpose in our lives. So, my recommendation to you is to reject the null and to accept the alternative, God's alternative, for your life.

I am rejecting the null! I am claiming God's unfathomable favor! We find a new purpose with unreasonable faith that defies logic—unexplainable, unreasonable faith, latent faith. The panacea, the prescription for fulfilling your purpose with relentless favor. Unwavering faith that defies logic! In my journey of faith and fulfillment, finding that hidden purpose, fulfilling my ultimate dream, purpose, and passion, I am finding that my purpose in using unrelenting faith—defiant, daring, and determined as a destiny chaser, using relentless faith.

God has the final say—as I find God's purpose for my life, I am reminded that God has the final say!

I am trusting the still, small voice. I am destined to find faith, favor, and determination in the journey of transition and transcendence. I know that my destiny is determined by the Creator, the arbiter of my faith. I am guided by the God who threw the stars in space and holds the world in the palm of His hands. I am vindicated by the God who has worked all things out for my good.

I reach out to fulfill my destiny and purpose. I challenge you to do the same, knowing that *all* things work together *for your good!*

Bibliography

n.d.

Achor, Shawn. n.d. *The Happiness Advantage.*

Angelou, Maya. n.d.

Beckwith, Michael. n.d.

Bergland. 2017. "Neurogenesis vs neuroplasticity."

Blanton, Hart, and Elif. G. Ikizer. 2019. "Elegant Science Narratives and Unintended Influences: An Agenda for the Science of Science Communication." Social Issues and Policy Review 154-181.

Brown, Brene. 2013. "Vulnerability."

Brown, Les. n.d.

Canfield, Jack. n.d.

Carlyle, Thomas. n.d. "Great man theory."

Cesar, Shirley. n.d.

Chole, Alicia Britt. n.d. Anonymous.

Covey, Stephen. n.d. *7 habits of highly effective people.*

Crawford, Beverly. n.d.

Creswell, J.W. 2016. "Qualitative Inquiry and Research Design: Choosing Among Five Approaches." Thousand Oaks, CA: Sage.

Crosby, Fanny. n.d.

Dyer, Wayne. n.d.

Dyer, Wayne. n.d.

Earp, S. D. Golden and J. L. 2012. "Social ecological approaches to individuals and their contexts: twenty years of health education and behavior health promotion interventions." *Health Education & behavior* 364-372.

Ehrmann, Max. n.d.

Einstein, Albert. n.d.

Frankfort, C., & Nachmias, D. 2008. "Research methods in the social sciences."

Gay, L. R. 1996. "Educational Research: Competencies for Analysis and Application." New Jersey: Merrill.

Giants, David and the. n.d. "Stumbling Block to stepping stone."

Gladwell, Malcolm. 2000. *Tipping Point*. Boston New York London: Little Brown and Company.

Goleman, Daniel. 1995. "Emotional Intelligence."

Jakes, T. D. n.d.

Jameson, Alan. 2017. "Deep Trench Snailfish."

Jeremiah, David. n.d.

Johnson Oatman, Jr. n.d. "Higher Ground."

Laub, Robert J. Sampson and John H. n.d.

Mandela, Nelson. n.d.

Marley, Bob. n.d.

Newton, Isaac. n.d.

Nichols, Lisa. n.d.

Northridge, A. and Schultz, M. E. 2004. "Social Determinants of Health: Implications for Environmental Health Promotion." *Health Promotion & Behavior* 455-471.

Ross, L.D. & Nisbett, R. E. 1991. "The person and the situation: Perspectives of social psychology." New York: McGraw-Hill.

Rushnell, Squire D. n.d. 2001.

Sampson, Robert. n.d.

Seuss, Dr. n.d.

Smith, Michael W. n.d. Accessed 1998.

Sorkin, Aaron. 1992. "A few ghood men."

Twain, Mark. n.d.

White, Ellen G. n.d. *Desire of Ages*. New York: Pacific Press.

Williamson, Marianne. n.d.

About the Author

Dr. Karen A. Armstrong was born in St. Catherine, Jamaica. She earned her PhD in nursing from Georgia State University and holds a Master of Public Health in epidemiology from Emory University, as well as a Master of Arts in gerontology from Georgia State University. Dr. Armstrong earned a BS in psychology and a BSN from Kennesaw State University. Dr. Armstrong has over seventeen years of clinical experience. She is a member of Sigma Theta Tau, the international nursing honor society.

Dr. Armstrong inspires positive change and demonstrates passion, commitment, and dedication to the success of her students and programs. She resides in Atlanta with her husband of twenty-seven years, Winston, her two children, Shenelle and Shane, and a fur baby, Lila. She is an avid Scrabble player and loves to read, listen to music, dance, travel, practice yoga, go on nature walks, and binge watch TV.

Most of all, Dr. Armstrong loves to praise and worship. A woman of faith, she epitomizes strength, courage, and perseverance. She is a testimony to the fighting spirit. Further, she is quick to remind others that *all things work together for our good!*

Notes

Today I have come full circle. I am tenure track faculty at the university where I was told I would not make it. The University where I obtained two degrees. To God be the glory! All things work together for good to them that love God, to them who are called according to His purpose.

Endnotes

[i] without faith it is impossible to please Him (Hebrews 11:6 KJV)

[ii] I can do all things through Christ who strengthens me (Philippians 4:13 NKJV)

[iii] God has a master plan for my life (Jeremiah 29:11 KJV)

[iv] I am more than a conqueror through Christ (Romans 8:37 KJV)

[v] Like the Apostle Paul says in Romans 8:28 (KJV)—All things work together *for my good!*

[vi] With God, all things are possible (Mark 9:23 and Matthew 19:26 KJV)

[vii] God's will supersedes everything in all my affairs (Matthew 6:10 KJV)

[viii] my destiny is determined by the Creator, the arbiter of my faith (Genesis 1:16 KJV)

[ix] the King James Version of the Bible (Psalm 51:5) depicts people who are imperfect, undeserving

[x] weapons of warfare may be deployed, but they will not prosper (Isaiah 54:17 KJV)

[xi] I can do all things through Christ (Philippians 4:13 KJV)

[xii] The Apostle Paul (Philippians 3:8, 13-14 KJV) tells us that he counts all things loss except for the excellence of the knowledge of Jesus Christ, and we should forget the things that are behind us and

press toward the mark of the high calling of God in Christ

[xiii] rejoice always, pray without ceasing, and give thanks in all circumstances (1 Thessalonians 5:16-18 ESV)

[xiv] to obey is better than sacrifice (1 Samuel 15:22 KJV)

[xv] He can do exceedingly abundantly above all that we ask or think (Ephesians 3:20 KJV)

[xvi] The Bible says to forgive 70 x 7 (Matthew 18:22 KJV)

[xvii] for I know the plans I have for you, plans to prosper you and not to harm you, plans to give you hope and a future (Jeremiah 29:11 NIV)

[xviii] The Bible (1 John 4:18 NKJV) tells us that perfect love casts out all fear

[xix] The Bible tells us to keep thoughts that are true, honest, just, lovely, and things are of good report (Philippians 4:8 KJV)

[xx] All things work *for my good* according to Romans 8:28 (KJV)

[xxi] Max Ehrmann exquisitely articulates, "...you are a child of the universe, no less than the trees and stars, you have a right to be here. And whether or not it is clear to you, no doubt the universe is unfolding as it should..."

[xxii] the characteristics of the virtuous woman in Proverbs 31:15-17 (KJV): she would rise before daybreak and pray; she was ever on her knees interceding for all her family and friends and strangers.

xxiii the characteristics of the virtuous woman in Proverbs 31:15-17 (KJV): she would rise before daybreak and pray; she was ever on her knees interceding for all her family and friends and strangers.

xxiv the characteristics of the virtuous woman in Proverbs 31:15-17 (KJV): she would rise before daybreak and pray; she was ever on her knees interceding for all her family and friends and strangers.

xxv Like David, the Psalmist (Psalm 23 KJV), he was a man after God's heart (Acts 13:22 KJV)

xxvi Like David, the Psalmist (Psalm 23 KJV), he was a man after God's heart (Acts 13:22 KJV)

xxvii The Bible says "Do not touch the Lord's anointed..." (1 Chronicles 16:22 NKJV)

xxviii All things work together for good, as the Bible says (Romans 8:28 KJV)

xxix God has a way of reminding us that He is in control and does whatever He pleases (Psalm 115:3 NKJV)

xxx without faith it is impossible to please God (Hebrews 11: 6 KJV)

xxxi Zechariah 2:5 (NASB) says, "I will be a wall of fire around her, and I will be the glory in her midst."

xxxii Like Paul, I can say I have fought the good fight and finished the course (2 Timothy 4: 7 KJV)

xxxiii Like Jabez (1 Chronicles 4:10 NKJV), I can pray for God to enlarge my territory and bless me indeed

[xxxiv] Forgetting those things which are behind me I reach for to those things which are before me—I press toward the mark of the high calling which is in God and Christ Jesus (Philippians 3:13-14, KJV)

[xxxv] As we are told in Philippians 4:11 (KJV), I am content in whatever circumstance I find myself

[xxxvi] Joshua says to be strong and courageous, for the Lord our God is with us (Joshua 1:6, 9 KJV)

[xxxvii] We are told in 1 Corinthians 2:9 (KJV) that eyes have not seen, nor ears heard all the marvelous things the Lord has in store for His people

[xxxviii] Nothing is impossible when we put our trust in God (Luke 1:37 KJV)

[xxxix] The Bible tells us to ask and we shall receive, seek and we will find (Matthew 7:7 KJV)

[xl] The Bible (John 10:10 KJV) tells us, "I have come that [you] may have life and... have it more abundantly."

[xli] The Bible talks about not touching His anointed and doing His people no harm (1 Chronicles 16:22 KJV)

[xlii] Psalm 139:14 (KJV) says I am fearfully and wonderfully made

[xliii] Nothing happens to me without His approval or permission (Matthew 6:10 KJV)

xliv The Bible says without faith it is impossible to please God (Hebrews 11:6 KJV)

xlv I can do all things through Christ (Philippians 4:13 KJV)

xlvi Philippians 4:13 (KJV) reminds us that we cannot put our confidence in our talents, mental or physical prowess, spiritual or educational training—we can only place our confidence in God, the source of all gifts and blessings